# ABOUT THE AUTHOR

Dr Simon Raybould started his career as a research scientist looking at the causes of childhood cancers. He spent more than two decades in research, gaining an international reputation and being published in a remarkably wide range of journals. The greater part of his research was directly policy-orientated and he became interested in how scientific research is communicated, explained and applied (or not!). To that end, he left research to concentrate on explaining research to people in the 'real world' so that they can benefit from what scientists already know but haven't got around to telling people!

Now, Simon is a full-time trainer, specializing in helping people make better presentations. He's worked throughout the UK and abroad, with clients ranging from solo entrepreneurs to top staff at Dunlop and Dell Computers and from NHS personnel to politicians and researchers.

Simon's varied and unconventional career path has included working as a teacher (though not very much and for not very long); as an actor, playwright and author; as a lighting designer, specializing in dance productions; and as a fire-eater!

An adopted Geordie, Simon lives in the North-East with his wife, Corinne, and two daughters.

'There is no presentation this book wouldn't improve. Whatever your experience of presenting and whoever your audience, this book will make you a better presenter.'

**Paul McGee – The Sumo Guy, international speaker and bestselling author**

'This book is an invaluable aid to anyone who wants to be sure to get information of any type across to audiences of all sizes. The author has managed to distil detailed, complex scientific evidence into manageable and accessible chapters, with a wealth of further information clearly signposted at the end of each. From managing presentation nerves to ensuring audience understanding and retention of information, from font and animation advice to content management, the author has brought together every aspect of successful presentations in one place. An invaluable read for anyone interested in refining and improving their presentation technique, no matter how experienced they are.'

**Dr Joanna Berry – Director of External Relations at Newcastle University Business School**

'What a great little book! There is something here for everyone. Experts will find new ideas (and some science) to test and polish their performances; novices will get a flying start with a whole range of presentation skills, which the rest of us had to learn by trial and error. Simon Raybould's accessible and charming writing style makes you feel as though you are having personal expert tuition.'

**Peter Judge, MBE, Attorney General of the Falkland Islands and South Georgia and the South Sandwich Islands**

# PRESENTATION GENIUS

40 insights
from the
science of
presenting

SIMON RAYBOULD

1                 658.452

Also available in ebook

# CONTENTS

# ACKNOWLEDGEMENTS

It's hard to know where to start: as any writer knows, just because it's your name on the front it doesn't mean you did all the work.

Before getting to the personal thank yous, it's important to recognize the people whose work I report here... the researchers (and their subjects!) who explore how the world (and the people who live in it) works. Without your efforts, your integrity, your intelligence and your rigour, this would be a book of opinions only.

I spent well over two decades as one of you before I left, and I know how damned hard you work. It's a great feeling to sit there at two o'clock on a Thursday afternoon, when your research finally works, to realize you now know something no one else in the world knows, but it's quite another thing to sit there at two o'clock that morning as you bash your head against some stubbornly impossible analysis results or impossibly dirty data (again!).

Moving on to the personal thank yous, I can only say a gentle prayer of gratitude to Corinne. Not just for your love and support while I wrote this book (and your work *on* the manuscript!) but for all the 30 years beforehand. May we have many, many more. You managed to stay wonderful even when I was snarling about how you were wrong. For the record, usually you weren't.

I also need to say a huge serious thanks to Clare Andrews for, well, more or less everything. You worked so very hard to improve my script and keep your 'suggested' changes in line with my style. (I may even, eventually, forgive you for some of the feedback comments.) If people like this book it is in no small measure because of you. Of course, if you don't like it...

I'm also very much indebted to Antoinette Oglethorpe, Dinah Bennet, Lesley Hunter and Craig Smith of my mastermind group, who slapped me around the face with a wet fish at one particular meeting and told me to get on with things. Without you guys I wouldn't even have started.

Karen Laing and Lydia Bates deserve the credit for helping me find some of the material, too. A mastery of search tools is a fine thing to see, especially when they're using it to make your life easier. Andrew Sommerville of SportScotland's Institute of Sport went out of his way to pass me some great sources and leads, as did Martin Wilson at TIN Arts and Amanda Drago of Arts Council England. And I couldn't forget Mike Dain. Big thank yous to all.

And another thanks to Stever Robbins (see his 'Get things done' blog http://www.quickanddirtytips.com/get-it-done-guy), not least for podcasting just the right thing at the right time.

I'm grateful to everyone who has commented on the content and greatly value their input, thoughts and sage recommendations. I hope the finished book serves their contributions well.

And it almost goes without saying that I'm thankful to you, too, for reading the finished product. (I'm even more grateful if actually you paid for it.)

# INTRODUCTION

## Where is this book coming from?

Early on in its creation (the stage my elder daughter would call 'idea-ing') this book was called 'The Science of Presenting', so it seems odd to write an introduction that is based upon a personal belief rather than a scientific fact. But for what it's worth, here it is: 'Presentations aren't (just) **about** something, they're a rallying call to **do** something.' Or, to be more pretentious about it...

*A presentation should change the world* (or at least your little bit of it).

If all you're doing is *telling* people things, there are generally better ways of doing it. If something doesn't change as a result of your presentation, you've just 'performed' an expensive waste of time, energy and money. What's worse, it's not just your own time, energy and money that you've wasted but that of every member of your audience, too. And it's probably been quite stressful as well.

**This book is intended to help you make presentations that are more effective – in other words, presentations that change things.**

With just one unfortunate exception (when you have to make a presentation simply because your boss tells you to), I'm willing to bet that you *don't* tell people about the new tax regulations for the sake of it: you tell them so that they abide by them. You *don't* tell people about your charity for the sake of it: you tell them so that they'll support you. You *don't* tell people about your new business idea for the sake of it: you tell them so that they'll promote you. You *don't* tell people about... you get the idea, I'm sure.

The best man at a wedding doesn't say things for the sake of it. He does it because he wants people to have a good time, and because he wants the bride and groom to know how much they are loved.

Martin Luther King didn't say 'I have a dream' because he liked the sound of his own voice (although he might well have done). He said 'I have a dream' because he wanted equal rights in the United States.

The important thing is that each and every presentation has a point to it – something that needs to change. Presumably it's something about your audience, such as an action they take, or an attitude they have, or a belief they hold… but there is always going to be something.

A few things follow on from this personal belief:

More recently Steve Jobs, the adulated CEO of Apple, gave famous 'keynotes'. They weren't given for the sake of his ego: he gave them to increase the sales of Apple products.

Potential entrepreneurs on *Dragon's Den* don't make presentations because they are fun (lots of them look like they're not enjoying it at all!). They make them because they want the Dragons to invest in them and their ideas.

- as a presenter you need to know the real aim of your presentation – so you can make it more likely that you hit that target
- presentations aren't about telling people what *you* know – they're about telling them what *they* need to know, in the way *they* need to know it.

This book helps you do that. In particular it helps with the second of those two statements.

What follows inevitably from the second bullet point (the idea that you tell people what they need to know in the way they need to know it) is that presentations aren't always the right thing to do. If the best way to change something is a presentation, then great, this book is going to help you – but if the best way is to bring in a raft of synchronized swimmers then put this book down and hire yourself some swimmers!

Some years ago I learned to waltz, in secret, as a surprise for my wife on our 25th wedding anniversary. It worked – she hadn't a clue it was coming and there wasn't a dry eye in the room – but the point is that the wonderful lady who taught me didn't do it by making a presentation.

She did it by putting my hands where they should be, and moving my feet. It was what I needed to know in the way I needed to know it.

Of course, in the real world you probably have to make presentations even if you know it's not the best approach – and this book will help with that, too!

## But why a book on presentations, specifically?

Often, giving presentations is about as popular as paying taxes. We all know we've got to do it but sometimes we wish we didn't.

And sometimes our audiences wish we hadn't.

There's a whole stack of books about presentations out there – and even more YouTube videos, websites, online courses, free downloads and, well... you name it. So why does the world need one more addition?

Because of the science behind it. What you're about to read about isn't based upon my experiences: it's based upon research. Not my research but university research. Research that's mainly published in peer-reviewed, high-impact academic journals. In other words: the gold standard of investigations.

This book is about making your presentations more effective and less stressful. It's about wasting less time on the boring, ineffectual things in presentations that give them (and you!) a bad name. I've been a presentation skills trainer for about ten years now but this isn't a book full of my experience and opinions. It's a book based upon some 400 pieces of research, much of it very, very new.

That's a lot of scientists doing a lot of research. Each chapter takes some of the cutting-edge (or in a few cases tried, true and longstanding) pieces of research related to presenting, communication or psychology – and even physics – and applies them to presenting, so that you can apply them to your own presentations.

# HOW TO USE THIS BOOK

Some of the chapters in this book relate to each other – and you'll find a 'See also' section at the end of each chapter - but I've written them to be more or less independent. That means you don't **need** to read them in a very specific order if you don't want to. The order they're in here represents the order in which I would read them but my needs are (by definition) different to yours. Feel free to jump around if you so wish.

Having said that, there are a few obvious groupings of chapters – for example, it makes little sense to read the third chapter about Professor Robert Cialdini's work without having read the first of them… but that's just common sense.

There is also a loose grouping of chapters that I've sketched out in the table that follows. You can use this to help you plan your reading if you so wish.

So why haven't I put the chapters in a 'sensible' order? Why haven't I created a structured 'course' out of the material here? Simply because I trust you to know your own needs better than I do – and in any case, see the chapter called **Back to school**.

At the end of each chapter you'll also find some **Further reading** in case you want to take things on a bit. I've deliberately gone off on a bit of a tangent with some of these, so imagine me with a wry smile as I add them. You should also know that a lot of the **Further reading** ideas are for videos or similar resources rather than literal reading – they tend to be a lot lighter than the references I've used for the book itself. No doubt each one will take you off on your own individual journey and that's fine!

Don't get put off by the sheer volume of information about presenting, either. If I'm feeling cynical I'd suggest you simply remember you don't need to be a presentation genius to be better than most people. Consider the old joke about two people running from a lion? One says to the other: 'This is ridiculous,

you can't outrun a lion' at which point the other one says:
'I don't need to outrun the lion – I just need to outrun you!'.

That said, I hope you want to be a better presenter for all the right reasons. There are hundreds, if not thousands of reasons for wanting that, but I'm going to sum it all up in one go:

Why should you want to be a better presenter? Because of your audience. It's that simple, really.

## Continuing the conversation

As I wrote this book, I tended to envisage it as my side of a conversation – answering questions that you'd not had the chance to ask. (Don't worry, the questions had been asked on your behalf by the very many people who've asked for help or who've come on my training courses.)

Why would you want to carry on a conversation? Because research moves on.

For example, the very last thing I did before I wrote this Introduction was to read about some research that won't be published until a couple of months after this book hits the shelves, but which would have fitted nicely into a couple of chapters. I hope you find this book a great stepping stone, but remember there is always going to be something new…

If you'd like to carry on this conversation, you're welcome to do so at presentationgenius.info. It would be great to meet you, and though I can't promise I'll answer each and every person individually I'll certainly do my best to make it a useful place for you.

| How people learn | How to get yourself ready | Tools you can use | Techniques you can use in your design |
|---|---|---|---|
| You know that feeling when your head is full... | Fashionable fear | It's grim up north | The vexed picture question |
| Overloaded | Minding what you say | Power of persuasion | ☞ ♄ ♗ ❄ ♦ |
| Back to school | Getting to bed | Being more persuasive | Doctors know best |
| Learning styles | Fit to talk? | Telling stories | Clarity is king |
| Why we can't remember long shopping lists easily (or is that just me?) | Being who you are | Being subtle | First things first |
| Chunking facts up | | Being judged | Story time |
| Writing down your wisdom | | Saying hello at the door | The best of PowerPoint® |
| Stay alert at the back | | Repeating yourself | Moving pictures |
| Blindness isn't in the eyes | | And more persuasive still | Put a record on |
| Blaming the right people | | Stand up! Stand up! | Diagram design |
| | | Knowing how good your presentation was | It's not what you say, it's the way that you say it |
| | | Fast and hard | |
| | | The Lucifer Effect | |
| | | Waving not drowning | |

# 1 FIRST THINGS FIRST

*Does the order in which you give information affect the way it's received?*

We know that first impressions are formed (quite naturally) very quickly. And we also know that once they're formed it's tough to change them. But does that tendency carry over from our audience's perception of us as presenters on to the information itself? Of course there's bound to be a relationship because if your audience thinks you're an idiot from the first impression, then they're unlikely to take your data seriously (and presumably if you create a good first impression your data is more likely to be trusted). But the question of how to *present* information is a slightly different one.

It's a question that's been of interest for a long time. After all, it has huge implications in, for example, court cases. If information presented to the jury in the early parts of a trial is discounted, the crucial piece of evidence should be saved for later, and so on.

Philip Tetlock looked at more or less this exact question back in the early 1980s. Working at the University of California, he was interested in the order in which information was presented and – importantly – how any effect it caused could be mitigated (or even *if* it could).

Psychologists have long known that information presented early in a debate weighed much more heavily than information presented later. Their term for this is the 'primacy effect'. The question of what causes it is complicated and there were competing early theories:

- getting bored or mentally tired; once we lose our concentration, new information can't be processed as well, no matter how much we want it to be, subconsciously assuming later information is implicitly less reliable
- becoming biased by the early information; information we receive later is interpreted in a way that means it backs up the assumptions we made based on early information (no matter how much twisting of the evidence we need to do for this).

As presenters, the cause is almost irrelevant – what matters is what we can do about it and how big the problem is. That said, of course, if knowing the cause helps stop the problem in the first place, it would be even better…

Tetlock's work also nicely addressed an additional question: does the primacy effect stay as strong if the stakes are raised – if people know they're going to be called upon to justify things after they've been given information, such as, hopefully, at work or in a court of law. The idea might be that knowing you're going to have to answer questions – with consequences for getting them wrong – might make people less sensitive to the primacy effect. There's some evidence already that people who expect to have to justify their opinions (to someone else whose opinion they didn't know) tended to be more nuanced about how they interpret data. People who had no such need to pay attention didn't, frankly; instead they relied much more upon the 'likeableness' of the source of the message. Both alternatives are important for a presenter, obviously.

To investigate all this, 72 undergraduates at the University of California were randomly grouped and given a booklet with instructions and a descriptive piece about a court case involving a death. There then followed a short piece of background information – just enough for them to understand the evidence that followed.

The evidence came after that – a set of 18 individual pages – half of which contained evidence supporting a guilty verdict and half of them with evidence supporting a verdict of not guilty. Each page only had one basic theme, to make it easier for people to assimilate the information: as you can imagine reading 18 pieces of information can be a little overwhelming, particularly as for this experiment people were given only about 30 seconds to read each page. (The similarities with how your audience receives information in presentations is pretty obvious, I'd say.)

To look at the question of whether or not having to justify yourself later had an effect, some volunteers were told that their impressions of the accused person would be confidential – and couldn't be traced to them. On the other hand, others were told they'd be asked to justify their impressions later. Still others were told this, but only after they'd read the information.

As you might guess, the booklets weren't all the same. There were three orders for how the pages were arranged:

- evidence of guilt followed by evidence of innocence
- evidence of innocence followed by evidence of guilt
- randomly ordered evidence, alternating between information suggesting guilt and that suggesting innocence.

After three minutes of thinking time, the volunteers were asked, bluntly: 'How likely do think it is that Smith killed Dixon?' and asked to score on a scale of 0 to 100 their confidence about a guilty verdict.

I'm sure you'll not be surprised to know there was a clearly visible and statistically significant primacy effect. In other words, when people were given the 'guilty' information first they were more likely to assume guilt and vice versa. (Those people given the data in random order fell neatly between the two other groups, reassuringly.)

Clearly the primacy effect is significant and as presenters it can make a real difference to how we order the information we give people. I think that's particularly likely to be the case if you're the kind of person who naturally wants to build up methodically and sequentially towards a final conclusion.

The second question remains, though. Does knowing that you'll have to justify yourself mitigate the primacy effect in any way?

The answer, in short, is a clear 'yes'. When data supporting innocence was presented first, all three groups (group 1: not accountable; group 2: told about being accountable up front; and group 3: told about being accountable only after the data was presented) had a relatively low, and similar, guilty score. For all three groups the guilty score was highest for when guilty-related data was presented first – but, interestingly, people who were told they would be held accountable for their opinion right at the start of the process were much less likely to go for a guilty score, followed by group 2, the told-about-being-accountable-later group (let's just call them the 'later' group) and the no-accountability group. In fact, group 1 was so much less likely to go for a guilty verdict than the other two groups that the immediate conclusion is that people in the 'later' group and the 'no accountability' group went through the same relatively superficial process of looking at the data and only group 1 really paid much attention to the information.

I can only imagine the feeling of panic that ensued when the 'later' group realized they would be asked to account for themselves after all…

There's another big implication for presenters that comes from this research. When they were asked about the information they had been given, volunteers who had been told at the very start that they'd be asked to justify themselves could remember a lot more of that information – information both supporting guilt and supporting innocence. It's hard to avoid the conclusion that they had simply paid more attention to the information, whichever verdict it supported – not least because the 'later' group could remember no more of the information they'd been given than the 'no accountability' group.

As presenters, the implications are fairly obvious. No matter what it is we want our audiences to remember, whether they agree with us or not, they're more likely to remember it if they feel some form of responsibility, such as knowing they're going to be asked questions to justify themselves. Personally, I find the idea of warning my audience that they 'need to take notes because there will be a quiz at the end' horrible, no matter how subtle or sophisticated it is. It treats people like children who don't want to learn.

Your circumstances will be different, of course, depending on the people you're talking to and how eager they are to hear what you've got to say, but my preference is to spend some of my time on stage (whether that's a literal stage or just the couple of spare metres at the front of your company boardroom) exploring with the audience why whatever-I'm-talking-about is important and, in particular, why it's important for them: that is, you show them how they are accountable for remembering what you say, simply because it has implications for their own benefit and lives.

## So what are the big takeaways here?

- **Present your big, powerful arguments first.**
- **Make it clear to your audience that they are responsible for the judgements they make about the information and arguments you're going to give them.** Remind them that they will have to justify their behaviour after this presentation and make them feel some responsibility for making the right decisions and doing the right thing.
- **Make yourself, your message and the way you deliver it as 'likeable' as you can.** This can include the obvious things such as how you dress and how you speak, but also the neatness of your slides, how easy to read and understand they are and how much fuss and faff there is involved – the less the better.

## Source

Tetlock, P. E. (1983), 'Accountability and the Perseverance of First Impressions', *Social Psychology Quarterly*, Vol. 46 No. 4 pp 285–92

## See also

Chapter 6 – The 'Assert-Evidence' approach to slide design also looks at the order in which you give information. See **It's not what you say, it's the way that you say it**

## Further reading

Is it possible to have better debates? This video suggests it's tricky but possible: http://www.ted.com/talks/michael_sandel_the_lost_art_of_democratic_debate

When it comes to maths, there's some idea that the order in which information is presented makes the question more (or less) easily solved. The abstract is free but you may need to pay for the full article: http://onlinelibrary.wiley.com/doi/10.1111/j.1949-8594.1964.tb14814.x/abstract

# 2 YOU KNOW T
# FEELING WH
# YOUR HEAD IS
# FULL...

*When and why does your audience get saturated?*

I don't know about you, but back in the days when I was doing pure research, my boss would sometimes comment, accurately, that my 'shutters had come down'. What he meant was that my brain had reached saturation and even though I was physically in the office, I might as well not be. A less polite way of putting it was: 'the lights are on but nobody's home'. So what had happened?

I'd got to the point where I couldn't think any more – my brain was full. My job was 'research' and I would have been working on a problem until the problem got the better of me. Temporarily, usually.

Usually.

Back in the early 1980s there was a big thing about solving problems and the big idea that grew out of all the research was that of Cognitive Load Theory (CLT). CLT takes the idea that we've all got limited working memory (or processing power) available and we use it to do two things at the same time, when we're solving a problem. The first is, obviously, solve the problem: the second thing is to learn from the problem, generalize it and develop a 'schema' so that we recognize that sort of problem in the future and don't have to do things from scratch all over again.

Pretty obviously, if we've got a fixed upper limit on our working memory, the more effort we're putting into the first of those tasks eater cognitive load) the less capacity we've got for doing e latter. I think that's important to presenters because I don't just want people to respond to me at that time, in that room. Sure, it's great if they understand me, are entertained and agree with the ideas I'm giving them, etc., but the real test of whether a presentation is a success is how many of my audience take what they've been given and apply it in their version of the 'real world'.

Doing that means they need to develop a personal schema because it's remarkably unlikely that their working life will be exactly the same as yours.

John Sweller is one of the big names in this field and as long ago as 1988 he was reporting experiments using school pupils in New South Wales, Australia, in the journal *Cognitive Science*.

Sweller observed that one of the key differences between experts and novices in how they solved problems was that experts didn't need to work things out backwards from the end point: they simply started to work forwards from where they were towards where they wanted to be. This wasn't due to differences between the expert and the novice in the ways you might expect – but largely to do with the way that experts could recognize patterns based upon the relevant schemas.

For example, novices tended to group problems according to how they are presented but experts do so based upon how that problem can be solved – in other words, they see past the superficial details because of their experience. Schemas are simply the tools they use for building that experience.

With that in mind it's pretty clear that anything that helps novices develop schemas is a good thing. The obvious tool at the presenter's disposal for doing this is to reduce the cognitive load they put on their audience during the presentation: that frees them up to spend more of their 'brain power' on linking the content of the presentation back to their lives. As Sweller says: 'Under most circumstances, means-ends analysis will result in fewer dead-ends being reached than any other general strategy which does not rely on prior remain-specific knowledge for its operation. One price paid for this efficiency may be a heavy use of limited cognitive-processing capacity.'

Sweller's experiment in this paper was beautifully simple. He already knew that traditional problem-solving in mathematics (such as 'solve for X' or 'calculate Y') led to more mathematical errors compared to a group of students who were simply given non-specific tasks such as 'figure out all the values you can' and he built on this to look at memory and learning, not just how well pupils performed with fewer cognitive demands placed on them. Some 24 students were given a series of mathematical problems involving working out the lengths of lines and sizes of angles in triangles, after they'd been taught how to use sine, cosine and tangent ratios.

Half the students were told to solve a specific question, while the other half were told simply to find the lengths of as many sides as they could... and, after each problem, everyone had to re-create, as far as they could, the information in the previous problem, not the one they had just solved. Some interesting things came out when they looked at the results.

First, the non-specific group was marginally quicker for each problem (but only marginally) and, although both groups got better as they did more of the problems, there was no statistically significant difference between the error rates. Nor were there differences between the two groups in terms of how long they took to re-create the previous problem (... and again both groups got faster).

So far, so disappointing.

But things got interesting when Sweller looked at the thing he was actually interested in – retention. For all six measures of error (things like correctly labelling the sides or calculating the angles between them) the group that hadn't been given a specific problem to solve – and therefore had a lower cognitive load – made fewer errors. In other words, when students weren't burdened by the need to 'get it right' they learned more.

In Sweller's own words:

- 'More excess capacity appears to be available after solving a non-specific goal problem than a conventional problem'
- 'Conventional problem-solving activity via means-ends analysis normally leads to problem-solution, not to schema acquisition'.

There are a few teachers I remember from my schooldays who might want to take note of that.

The implications for presenters are huge. If we make our audiences work too hard, so that they're struggling to understand what we're saying, they're less likely to remember things after the end of the presentation – and if they can't remember it I think it's less likely they'll apply it. As I've said before, application is what it's about, for me.

That means that anything we can do to allow our audiences to concentrate on our material without having to worry about other things can be handy. While it's important for audiences to see why your material matters to them, there's a balance to be struck. If all you do is work through the solution to one problem, that's all your audience will know.

It also means you should think about removing anything from your presentation that isn't relevant. If your audience is concentrating on fripperies or trying to see how an irrelevant piece of information relates to the big picture (when it doesn't), you'll reduce the amount of cognitive capacity they've got available to concentrate on the real core of your presentation.

Taking this one step further, you might find it handy to deal with anything you can think of that might chip away at your audience's cognitive capacity. With my tongue only slightly in my cheek, things that I've noticed in presentations over the past month (there are others, of course, this list is just based on what I noted down recently) include:

- irrelevant material – everything you say is processed by your audience and they've only got a limited amount of attention to give you, so don't risk spreading it too thinly
- what you're wearing – colourful, large, garish or unusual ties, earrings and so on are more distracting than you might think
- jargon – if people are having to 'translate' your slides they've got less capacity to concentrate on the contents
- the temperature of the room – people thinking about how cold it is aren't fully paying attention
- how long it is to the next break – anyone worried about getting something to eat or drink has less capacity to concentrate on you
- hard-to-read fonts – if people need to work hard to figure out what the slides *say* they won't be able to concentrate on what they *mean*.

It's all pretty obvious, really, but it's nice when science and our prejudices tell us the same thing, isn't it!

## So what are the big takeaways here?

- **Don't get too complicated, so that your audience struggles to understand what you mean.** If in doubt, keep it simple and talk about the ideas, not the details. Let people know where they can get hold of the details from (and make sure they can).
- **Provide plenty of 'hooks' for your audience to see how what you're saying applies to their working environments.** Examples and case studies are a good bridge between what you're saying and what they experience, but don't be over-specific. Some people will have difficulty translating a very detailed example into their world.
- **Strip away everything you can that distracts from what you're trying to say.** Brutally remove irrelevant information and see if you can deal with the distractions of the room. If people are thinking about how long it is to the next coffee break they aren't concentrating on the information of the presentation, so make sure everyone knows. You might consider housekeeping irrelevant compared to the world-changing great disclosures you're making, but your audience might not.

## Source

Sweller, J. (1988), 'Cognitive Load During Problem Solving: Effects on Learning', *Cognitive Science* Vol. 12 pp 257–85

## See also

Chapter 4 – To help people feel familiar with even new material, and reduce cognitive load, try **Repeating yourself**

Chapter 12 – Getting the level of saturation wrong leads to your audience being **Overloaded**

Chapters 14 and 15 – People can only hold so much in their heads at once. See **Why we can't remember long shopping lists easily (or is that just me?)** and **Chunking facts up**

## Further reading

Garr Reynolds started what can only be described as a revolution in presentations with his Presentation Zen philosophy. The whole blog is dripping with good material, but you might be particularly interested in his look at cognitive load and presentation slides. It's at: http://www.presentationzen.com/presentationzen/2007/04/is_it_finally_t.html

I'm generally sceptical of blogs written by companies (my own excepted, of course!) but this one gives some good advice about using the cognitive load approach in presentations, see: http://www.ethos3.com/2015/01/how-to-minimize-the-extraneous-load-of-your-presentations

# 3 CLARITY IS KING

*The art of simplicity is a puzzle of complexity*

Every book on writing style that I've ever read, and every bit of advice I've ever been given, has been to clarify, simplify and to cut out all unnecessarily complicated words and phrases. (If I've not managed to do that in this chapter, kindly keep that opinion to yourself…) Unfortunately, like more or less everyone I know, I've been guilty of trying to boost my perception of myself by boosting the syllable count of some of my writing. I did it as an undergraduate a long time ago but I like to think I do it less now.

The big, important question is, basically 'does it work?' Does using a more convoluted sentence structure or more polysyllabic words make me look and sound smarter? That's the very question addressed by Daniel M. Oppenheimer of Princeton University in a paper with a title that surely should win an award: 'Consequences of Erudite Vernacular Utilized Irrespective of Necessity: Problems with Using Long Words Needlessly.'

Oppenheimer had an interesting starting-point: when undergraduates at Stanford were polled about how they wrote, more than 85 per cent of them admitted to using long words in an academic essay to make it sound better. In fact, nearly two-thirds of them *even used a thesaurus* to help the pick the words.

Presumably, our instinct to do this is based upon an instinctive recognition that people who are more intelligent tend to have larger vocabularies (there's research evidence of this) and so our internal logic runs that the opposite must be true as well. So why is it that expert advice always advocates the more simple approach? Possibly because of the research evidence: simpler writing is associated with a number of very positive concepts, including:

- truth and veracity
- confidence
- frequency (feeling familiar with things)
- fame
- liking.

Oppenheimer carried out some simple but effective experiments. The first looked at whether increasing the complexity of text made the author appear smarter. It also looked at whether any such effect was influenced by how complex the original writing was. To get at this, essays written for admission to graduate school were made more complex by substituting some of the original words with more complex alternatives, in fact with the longest word available based on thesaurus entries presumably on the assumption that longer words were more complex for readers. A 'highly complex' version of extracts from six personal statements was created and shown to 71 other students. A 'moderately complex' version was also created by simply substituting fewer words. The participants were asked to give a recommendation for whether to accept or reject the author and to score how confident they were about that on a scale of one to seven. If you convert the 'accept vs reject' to scores of +1 and −1, then weight them by the confidence score, you get a scale of −7 up to +7 and the results were pretty clear. Highly complex excerpts had an average score of −2.1: the 'moderately complex' excerpts had an average of −0.17 and the original excerpts had an average of 0.62.

In other words, even the moderate modifications meant that, on average, the authors would have been rejected! What's more, this effect held true even after the complexity of the original text had been taken into account.

Instead of making authors look smarter, increasing the complexity of text seems to make them look less intelligent.

The implications for presenters are pretty clear. Using clear and simple delivery of your material will make you look smarter (on average).

Not content with this result, a similar experiment used two different translations of the same original, foreign-language version. The idea behind this is that changing words, as had been done in the first experiment, might have been artificial in some way, making some sentences unreasonably clumsy. Two translations of some Descartes (Meditation IV) were given to undergraduates, who were given a week to complete questionnaires.

An extra dimension was added because half of the participants were told who wrote the original while the other half weren't. For those who knew where the original came from, Descartes was scored as more intelligent by those who read the more simple translation. Participants who didn't know who wrote the original (because they weren't told) also rated the 'simpler' author as smarter.

The results support the first experiment but – obviously – this might just be because of how well or badly translated the passages were... so on to experiment three. Building on the first experiment it seems reasonable to see if authors can be made to look smarter by simplifying their originals. The short answer is 'yes': comparing originals to simplified versions led to average opinions about the author's intelligence being higher for the simplified versions.

It's not necessarily easy to see a direct process by which all of this could work, but one possible way it could happen is because of 'fluency'. Better written material has more fluency, and so it's more accessible. If that's right, we might expect other things that mess up fluency to reduce how intelligent authors seem to be – and that's reasonably easy to test because different fonts are easier to read than others. All you have to do is prepare the same text in different fonts and see which gives the highest presumed intelligence for the author.

Oppenheimer used 12 point Times New Roman (the original version) and compared it to *Juice ITC font* – in italics, for good measure. By now it shouldn't come as any surprise to discover that the 'author' of the Times New Roman version of the document was believed to be more intelligent than the *Juice ITC* 'author'. *Juice ITC* is much harder to read, after all.

So where are we with all of this? Pretty clearly, we know that:

- a lot of non-experts tend to try to make themselves sound smarter by writing in more difficult, convoluted ways
- conversely, experts suggest that a better way to write is to be clear and concise, avoiding complicated and unnecessary words
- empirical evidence strongly suggests that the experts are right – because all other things being equal, readers assume that people are smarter when their writing is more simple, and less intelligent when their writing is complicated
- this effect is probably explained by the concept of fluency – the ease with which words are processed.

There are two other bits of information to take on board, too. First, when text has an ease of fluency the effect is multiplied when it is unexpected (that is, when people find things easier to grasp than they thought they would, the effect is greater); and, second, that when people believe the (lack of) fluency is not the author's fault (such as when it's just printed badly), they not only forgive the author but over-compensate, assuming better things about the author than they otherwise would.

So how can presenters use this? I think it's pretty simple and obvious. Be clear, be simple and be fluent. To me that includes clear, simple fonts, written in a size large enough to make it easy for your audience to read and so on. Diagrams can be simplified to show only the things your audience needs to see to help them understand. (You can add all the messy details later, if you need and want to, I suppose, once the audience has got the hang of the basics.)

## So what are the big takeaways here?

- **Big, clean, familiar and simple fonts are best.** Don't make your audience struggle to understand what you're writing, saying or drawing.
- **The easier you can make what you say, the smarter your audience will believe you to be, so keep your words short and**

simple. Personally, I find it handy to 'write' what I'm going to say by saying it out loud rather than by writing it down. My written stuff is more sophisticated than my spoken stuff – and I tend to use shorter words when I speak than when I write. I suspect most other people do, too.

- **If you're using slides, keep them simple.** Change your default mindset to 'remove', and look at each element of the slide – then ask how it justifies being there. If it can't be done, then cut it out. It's a change in mindset that sounds simple but can have very profound effects on your designs.

## Source

Oppenheimer, D. M. (2006), 'Consequences of Erudite Vernacular Utilized Irrespective of Necessity: Problems with Using Long Words Needlessly', *Applied Cognitive Psychology*, Vol. 20 pp 139–56

## See also

Chapter 1 – The sequence you provide information in also helps, not just how clearly you give it. See **First things first**

Chapters 20-22 – Clarity helps trust, which helps you influence your audience: see **Power of persuasion**, then **Being more persuasive** and **And more persuasive still**

Chapter 24 – Clarity is also one of the eight key principles in **The best of PowerPoint®**

## Further reading

This is quite a fun idea – replace long words with shorter ones, for simplicity: http://home.comcast.net/~garbl/stylemanual/words.htm

In terms of making things as simple as possible, some of the world's greatest minds have chipped in: http://www.goodreads.com/quotes/tag/simplicity

There are plenty of tools for determining how easy to read a document is. Try something similar on your own spoken words – perhaps by doing a readability test on a transcript of your presentation. Try starting here: http://en.wikipedia.org/wiki/Flesch%E2%80%93Kincaid_readability_tests

# 4  REPEATING YOURSELF

*Does repeating yourself help? Does repeating yourself help?*

I've done it, and I'm sure you have too. Ever found yourself saying in a conversation: 'I can't remember where I read it, but I remember something about...'. We're pulling a half-remembered piece of information out of the recesses of our memory. To be honest, I often can't generally remember if the thing I'm recalling was valid, fair, truthful, accurate or even reasonable – I just remember that it existed and not much else.

But the simple fact that I could remember it meant I had a familiarity with it – and what is familiar is trusted. Researchers have a term for this kind of thing: they call it the 'illusion of truth'. Basically, it means that things we are familiar with are things that we tend to trust and believe more than things that are new to us.

> I'm speculating here, but there's a bit of me that thinks this makes very good sense, from an evolutionary perspective. After all, if it's familiar to us it means that at the very least it hasn't eaten us or killed us in some other way.

I'm not convinced of the absolute logic of this because it sounds to me a bit like buying a copy of a newspaper, not liking the headline, buying another copy of the same newspaper with the same headline and deciding to believe it the second time because I'm familiar with it. Whether it makes sense or not, we know it exists. In fact researchers have had evidence for it since the mid-1970s. What's more, the evidence isn't that we actually need to have seen something lots of times for the illusion of truth to work, we just need to feel as if we have.

What this means for presenters is that it's sometimes a good idea to package a novel concept in a familiar way. Giving me a brand-new idea using a brand-new technology might be too much for me, whereas giving me that very same idea using something I'm familiar with could be more successful. That's an argument for keeping the design of your slides relatively stable, or even just the very act of using slides rather than something else. (PowerPoint® vs Prezi®, for example.)

What's more, there's evidence that if something is easier to perceive it will tend to be regarded as more familiar than if it's harder to make out. The logic of that for presenters is that we should use colour schemes such as dark blue on white, rather than pale blue on white, simply because dark blue on white is easier to read.

If we take that idea one step further, our logic might be that things we can remember will seem more familiar, and thus feel more trustworthy precisely because we remember them (no matter what we felt about them at the time when we committed them to memory, perhaps). That was the area of interest of a couple of researchers from the University of Waterloo. In 2010 they reported some experiments that got right to the core of how much we trust things we remember. Their work took some setting up, so bear with me here.

Their idea was to give volunteers a set of carefully chosen factual statements, each one matched with an 'inference' statement. The factual statement could support or refute the inference statement, for example: '79 per cent of babies are born on their due date' as the factual statement (for the sake of this experiment they didn't need to be true!), which was matched with the inference statement: 'Doctors are remarkably accurate in predicting the exact day a baby will be born.'

The way these factual statements were chosen was by creating a long list of them and asking volunteers to rank them from one to seven for how believable they were: the 24 statements used in the rest of the research were chosen because they had a believability score of 3.53 – that is, more or less half-believable.

Once these factual statements were picked they were shown to a different set of volunteers in four different ways. In the first group, the control, participants were shown the inference statements and the factual statement that went with it at the same time. In other words, this group had no chance of the illusion of truth because they'd not seen the statements before. The second group saw the factual statements twice: the second time was just as it was for the control group, but for this group they had been shown the factual statements once before. The third group was exactly the same, except that by the time they saw the inference statements together with the factual statements they'd already seen the factual statements three times. That is, they saw the factual statements a total of four times.

The fourth group was a little different. They were shown the factual statements in the same way as the second group, but when they were subsequently shown the inference statements they didn't get to see the factual statements again: they had to rely on their memories.

Still with me after all that set up? Hopefully this table will help.

| Group number | Preparation activity | Test activity | Total number of times the factual statements were seen |
|---|---|---|---|
| One (the control) | | Factual and inference statements were shown together. | Once |
| Two | Factual statements were shown once. | Factual and inference statements were shown together. | Twice |
| Three | Factual statements were shown three times. | Factual and inference statements were shown together. | Four times |
| Four | Factual statements were shown once. | Inference statements only were shown. | Once |

The actual test part of the experiment was remarkably simple: when the participants read the inference statement they were asked to score it from one to seven on how accurate it was. A score of one meant it was totally inaccurate and a seven meant it was highly accurate. There was also a quick check after all this to see if participants recognized newly presented factual statements, to check how reliably they could remember what they'd seen and – fortunately for the sake of this experiment – people proved very good at spotting the newcomers, suggesting that there had been little forgetting.

So what were the results? Remember that if the illusion of truth idea is valid, we'd expect that the factual statements (which were chosen to be only half-believable) would cause a trend towards thinking the inference statements were accurate… and that's exactly what happened. In all of the last three groups, people were more inclined to mark the inference statements as accurate. It looks like the illusion of truth is validated, but we can unpack things a bit by comparing the three different experimental groups to each other as well as to the first (control) group.

Group two, who only saw the factual statements once before the test, did show a shift towards trusting the inference statements, but it wasn't statistically significant (that is, it could have been due to chance). But for group three, who had seen the factual statements three times before the test, there was a very clear tendency to think that the inference statements were accurate. The implication is that the illusion of truth is very real, but it needs a threshold number of exposures to things before it cuts in: it didn't happen for two exposures but it did for four.

From a presenter's point of view, the way to use this is simple. Repeat yourself. Make sure your audience is exposed to things relatively early in your presentation, so that you can re-expose them to those ideas later on. That might be as simple and bold as telling them what you're going to say, then providing the evidence in support of that claim, and then reminding them of what you've shown. Alternatively, you might want to be a bit more subtle and creative. Perhaps you might want to link things in your presentation to things that previous speakers have already said or slip in comments such as: 'As Dave told us last week...'. The key thing is that far from familiarity breeding contempt it looks like familiarity breeds trust.

However, there is one more group to look at – the final group. This is the group that was shown the factual statements once only, not even being shown them again when they were tested on their response to the inference statements. In other words, they had to rely on their memory of the 'facts'. Fascinatingly, this group showed differences to the control group at least as large as group three – who saw their facts a total of four times. In other words, pulling something out of memory was as effective as four repetitions. (I'm tempted to put that comment in a further three times, so that you trust it, but... )

What that means to you as a presenter is that you can build the effectiveness of your arguments simply by getting your audience to pull facts from memory. It might be something you've said earlier, or that someone else has said, or that they've seen and heard before your presentation begins...

Personally, I use this technique quite a lot by including 'flashbacks' to something I've said earlier but not giving people all the information – just enough for them to find what I'm talking about in their memories and recall it for themselves. An image from a previous slide might act as a stimulus, or a heading; the point is that they have to do the necessary mental work, not me.

... just don't repeat yourself to the point that you get boring, obviously.

## So what are the big takeaways here?

- Repeat yourself.
- Repeat yourself.
- Get your audience to think you've repeated yourself by making them pull things out of their memory as if you've repeated it.

## Source

Ozubko, J. D. & Fugelsang, J. (2011), 'Remembering Makes Evidence Compelling: Retrieval From Memory Can Give Rise to the Illusion of Truth', *Journal of Experimental Psychology: Learning, Memory and Cognition*, Vol. 37 No. 1 pp 270–6

## See also

Chapter 11 – For more on how to break things up for people, see **Back to school**

Chapters 20-22 – How much people trust you is also influenced by other things. See **Power of Persuasion** and the follow-on chapters

## Further reading

If you're a sci-fi fan, The Illusion of Truth is the name of an episode of *Babylon 5*, one of my favourites... http://www.imdb. com/title/tt0517706

There's a rather gory and vicarious illustration of the illusion of truth in this little video: http://vimeo.com/71671086

If you take the idea of the illusion of truth far enough, you end up with the concept of The Big Lie, a technique used by Hitler, among others, see: http://en.wikipedia.org/wiki/Big_lie

I might even suggest that the idea underlies most 'urban myths', made much more easy to spread because of the Internet: http://urbanlegendsonline.com

A lot of them can be debunked by a quick visit to: www.snopes.com

# 5 FAST AND HARD

*How quickly should you speak, and with how much passion?*

Whenever I ask people on my training courses what they want to look at, someone always –and I mean *always* – says that they speak too fast. My response is often to tell them not to worry about it, so long as they can be understood. And they're sceptical. They're sceptical because they're speaking fast (too fast, they think) because they're nervous and they've got the idea that slowing down will sort out their nerves… which is about as sensible as trying to treat BO with anti-perspirant: it takes a lot of effort and even if it works you're only dealing with the symptoms and not the cause.

Nevertheless, they say they want to slow down so that they sound more in control, but it seems I may have science on my side when I tell them to relax about things a bit. As far back as the mid-1970s researchers at the University of Southern California were looking into exactly this problem. They had noticed that a lot of people had looked at how well an audience *understood* a presenter speaking quickly, while very little work had been done on how easily an audience was *persuaded* by how quickly the presenter spoke.

> For the record, most studies didn't find any effect of the speed of delivery on the level of comprehension of the audience. As you might expect, however, under the specific circumstances where there was an effect, it was that the audience's comprehension was reduced.

That said, we might expect that if people don't understand you, they are less likely to be persuaded by you. After all, if people are persuaded by things they don't understand, something funny is going on (though it might explain a very great deal about politics and football, I suspect). On the other hand, an increase in the speed of delivery might mean that people don't have time to think of counterarguments to what they're being told and just get swept along with the flow. It might also be that slow speakers are seen as having to think too hard, leading to assumptions that they don't know their material. Speaking slowly might in fact reduce credibility.

The researchers reasoned that if speed caused a credibility issue, then variations in speed wouldn't make much difference to how the speaker was perceived (and in fact credibility might even go up with speed). Whereas if quick speaking worked because of its ability to ride rough-shod over the listener's critical capacity, there would be a negative reaction to different high speeds and that this reaction could get stronger as speeds increased. With that in mind, it was relatively easy to create experiments to test their thinking. (In fact, the researchers had already carried out some unpublished research and were fairly sure they knew what to expect – that speed is a credibility issue, not related to speaking faster than people can think to assemble counterarguments.)

In this research, assistant researchers posed as journalists from a radio station soliciting responses to a 'big issue of the day'. This 'big issue' was whether coffee was bad for you and – assuming agreement – a 400-word recorded article from the radio was played which made some pretty strong claims about the evils of coffee. In order to investigate whether speed and credibility of the speaker were related the recording was described as either of a biochemist (who presumably knew one end of a caffeine molecule from another) or a locksmith (who presumably didn't). At the same time, of course, some interviewees were played a low-speed recording of around 102 words per minutes or a high-speed recording at around 195 words per minute.

Afterwards the interviewee (by now no doubt anxious to get to their own next cup of coffee) was asked a few questions about how much they agreed with the content of the recording, how much the speaker knew about the subject, how clear they thought the recording was and – of course – their personal coffee-drinking habits.

If you've read other chapters, it'll come as no surprise to learn that the 'biochemist' was ranked as more knowledgeable, and also got higher scores for how easy to understand they were. This was by-the-by stuff for the researchers though, who were far more interested in the effects of speed of speech. The effects of speed on how knowledgeable the speaker was deemed to be were borderline, but generally the faster speaker was seen as more knowledgeable. What's more, when the amount of coffee drunk by the interviewee was factored in, the effect was clearer, but we might expect that; people agree with what they already believe.

Nothing seems to undermine credibility more than a speaker with long 'thought-pauses', except, perhaps, one whose thought-pauses are filled with 'Errrr'.

So far, so good. It appears I'm right to tell people not to worry about speaking quickly – it actually enhances their credibility and how you can use this information in your own presentations is pretty clear. I'm not advocating deliberately speaking quickly, simply that you don't need to worry about it if you do.

> If I'm right about why talking quickly boosts credibility – because it implies you know what you're talking about and aren't having to think about things too hard as you go along – one very clear additional tip for presenters would be to rehearse. Rehearse, rehearse, rehearse. Rehearse so that you know what you're going to say and can say it without having to stop too often to think.

I should add, at this point, that later work in this area has found a number of particular circumstances where the talking fast option is overruled by other things, but I've not worried about them here since they're covered in other parts of this book.

Knowing all this is very handy as a presenter, but it does raise some risks. If I'm in full flow I don't always stop to censor myself as much as I would if I were speaking more slowly and had time to think of the implications of what I'm saying. The chances of a faux pas of some kind might increase if I'm going at things full tilt and heaven protect me if, in my passion, I accidentally swear during a presentation. Or so the argument goes. In fact, the research in the area is more forgiving about the occasional lapse of judgement.

Obviously, it's hard to know exactly where the boundaries lie (I once was reprimanded for saying 'it's bloody hard work' in the middle of a presentation but I've heard other presenters use much stronger language), and you have to know your audience, but research from Northern Illinois University suggests that you can get away with at least a mild profanity – in fact you might even benefit from it as a speaker.

People swear for a lot of reasons, such as anger or joy, but one of the most common uses is to emphasize a feeling. With that in mind, perhaps the results of the following experiment aren't such a surprise. Eighty-eight students were shown a five-minute taped speech about lowering tuition fees at a different university. Some of the content was powerful stuff, some of it less so, but because they were already students and the tape wasn't about their university it was only mildly relevant to the participants.

Of course, this being an experiment, not all the students saw the same video. In fact they saw three different recordings which were, as far as possible, the same, except for one detail. In one video there was no swearing; in another the word 'damn' appeared near the start and in the third, the word appeared at the end. And as soon as the video was over participants were debriefed.

The videos with the swearing, in either position, had a significantly stronger effect on attitudes about the subject matter than the 'clean' video. That seems like a good thing to me, and something that presenters can use. However, there is the matter of whether swearing damaged the presenter's credibility and so on: analysis of the participants' responses showed that swearing had a positive effect upon the perceived intensity of the speaker and had absolutely no effect whatsoever on their credibility. In other words, swearing in this experiment had positive effects on audience outcome.

All of that said, don't come crying to me when someone heckles you: 'Potty Mouth'!

## So what are the big takeaways here?

- **Talk fast – or at least at your natural conversational speed –  rather than making a huge effort to speak slowly.** There's nothing to be lost, in terms of how well you'll be understood, and there's usually something to be gained in terms of your credibility.
- **Rehearse, or at least become familiar with your material in other ways, so that you don't stumble around, obviously thinking of what to say next.** Aim for a smooth flow of information.
- **Allow yourself to show a little passion** – even to the point of a mild profanity if you're reasonably confident your audience isn't going to be too offended.

## Sources

Miller, N., Maruyama, G., Beaber, R. J. & Valone, K. (1976), 'Speed of Speech and Persuasion', *Journal of Personality and Social Psychology*, Vol. 34 No. 4 pp 615–24

Scherer. C. R. & Sagarin, B. J. (2006), 'Indecent influence: The positive effects of obscenity on persuasion', *Social Influence*, Vol. 1 No. 2 pp 138–46

## See also

Chapter 26 – Of course, accents matter as well as how fast you deliver the words. See **It's grim up north**

Chapter 31 – Whatever you sound like, you're going to be judged by how you look as well. You're **Being judged**

## Further reading

The fastest speaking woman in the world is Fran Capo, at more than 600 words per minute: http://francapo.com/fastest-talker

While the record for the fastest man (more than 650 words per minute) is pretty old: https://www.youtube.com/watch?v=JEiFl8O5lV4

In *The Hitchhiker's Guide to the Galaxy* (what do you mean you've never heard of it!), the worst swear word conceivable was 'Belgium'. If you don't know 'the guide', start here: http://en.wikipedia.org/wiki/The_Hitchhiker's_Guide_to_the_Galaxy

# 6 IT'S NOT WHAT YOU SAY, IT'S THE WAY THAT YOU SAY IT

*Does the way you design your slides affect how much people remember?*

Few things in this world seem to be more fixed than how traditional university lectures are given. They've moved on from slides and acetate sheets to PowerPoint® presentations but the idea of just throwing information at the often stunned, benighted students hasn't changed much in some places. I like to think my lectures were a little different but I'm probably flattering myself. And with the advent of PowerPoint® and its default template came the idea of throwing that information at people in the form of nested sets of bullet points – without necessarily thinking through the question of whether or not that was the best way to deliver the information.

For me, delivering information has at least two components. First, you've got to deliver it to people so that they 'get it'; and second, you've got to find ways of making sure it stays in your audiences' heads. (The shorthand I often use for this is *penetration* and *retention* respectively.) It doesn't matter how much penetration your presentation gets if there's no retention.

Margaret V. Root Kustritz looked at how slide design affected both penetration and retention in third-year veterinary students. (By the third year we can reasonably expect them to know which way up a cow goes but there's still a lot for them to take in.) There was some voluntary element to how much the students got involved, but everyone had to get involved in one way or another – grades depended on it!

The basic idea of the research was simple: students were given the choice of when to attend what was, essentially, the same lecture. The evening version of the lecture was delivered using the traditional style of bullet points (T) and 31 of the 99 students involved came along to this. The next morning (in the usual 8 a.m. slot) the remaining students attended a version of the lecture using a different style of PowerPoint®, known as the **Assertive Evidence** method (AE). (The details are a bit messy and I'll go over them later in this chapter, but the main idea is simply to *find out* which of the two approaches meant that the students learned more and retained more). The table below summarizes the timetable and gives the results of the various tests that the students took based on this lecture.

Students were given a test at the start of the lecture to get a baseline measurement (and to make sure no one went to both lectures); following the lecture, they then had some work to complete at home, using freely available resources, with a two-week deadline and a pass mark of 15/25; and finally, a month later, the students were given the 'Retention Test' to see how much had stuck with them. To make sure that no one dropped out, they were told that the pass mark of 15/25 wasn't sufficient to pass – they also needed to have taken part in all the relevant tests.

Obviously, there's a bit of a problem here from a scientific point of view in that the students could decide for themselves which version of the lecture they went to and it's possible that better students went to the morning option (for example) but the similarity of the pre-test scores suggested this wasn't a problem in reality.

Incidentally, the students had all been given a learning styles test (see Chapter 33) before this work began. As you might expect having read that chapter, different learning styles had no statistical impact upon the results at all.

It's worth pointing out that while the difference of 0.7 between the two retention test scores doesn't sound like much that's nearly a full mark out of only ten available – not to be sneezed at – and it's in the context of an improvement of scores (above the original, starting point scores) of only around two out of ten. To be honest, my personal experience is that 'typical' business audiences learn and retain considerably less than that, which either says something about veterinary students compared to business audiences, or my presentations. I'm not going to speculate about which it is!

| Test | T lecture score averages (standard deviations) | AE lecture score averages (standard deviations) | Note |
|---|---|---|---|
| Pre-test given at the start of the lecture | 3.6 (1.6) | 3.7 (1.3) | A hard-copy multiple choice test of ten questions – the differences between the groups weren't significant |
| Take-home, open-source assessment | 23.7 (1.6) | 23.6 (1.5) | This was marked out of 25 and could be done at any time for two weeks after the lecture |
| Post-test | 6.2 (1.9) | 6.6 (2.0) | This was an online version of the same questions as in the pre-test: score differences aren't statistically significant |
| Retention test | 5.3 (1.8) | 6.0 (1.9) | This test had different questions to the pre- and post-tests but was in the same format: the difference in scores is statistically significant with only a 3 per cent chance of it being due to chance ($P = 0.03$) |

So what's the difference between the traditional lecture's use of PowerPoint® and the AE version of the lecture? Well the T version of the lecture was the typical 'death by PowerPoint®' of bullet points, often indented into a hierarchy – the kind that we're all too familiar with. The AE slides used the same font, colour scheme and so on, to make the comparison as fair as possible, but instead of the bullet points, AE slides contained:

- an assertion – in the form of a succinct headline sentence that gives the main point of the slide. It was left-justified and in a 28-point font, using the normal English traditions of capitalization and so on. At most, the assertion was two lines long
- the evidence – in the form of a highly relevant graphic – photographs rather than clip-art – which addressed the main point directly.

For example, instead of text about knee-joint problems (the T approach), an AE slide would contain a sentence about knee-joint problems and a picture of the problem in question. From a presenter's point of view, this approach is harder and needs more work, because it needs you to both:

- prepare the slides in a more time-consuming way that also takes more mental effort
- remember to say the things that you'd otherwise have written on your slide. However, given the evidence of this research (and the host of other articles that investigate similar things, all using slightly different methods in slightly different circumstances) it's an effort that is likely to be well worth your time.

One note of caution (born of personal experience)... it's easier to project text than to project images, particularly if they're complicated and in colour etc. Sunlight and badly positioned lights can make it harder for your audience to see what's on the screen, so make a point of checking that your images work when they're projected, not just that they look good on your computer screen.

And don't forget to make sure you've got the legal niceties out of the way, too. Just because you can download an image from the Internet doesn't mean you have the rights too!

## So what are the big takeaways here?

- **Use the AE guidelines of a single sentence,** supported by spoken detail and a large, clear and very relevant graphic, keeping to only one concept per slide.
- **Explore using Presenter View in PowerPoint®.** This allows you to see notes about the slide that your audience don't see and will help you to remember what it is you need to say in response to the slide. One of the advantages of the T approach is that the slides could work as a script for the presenter, whereas AE slides don't. Putting notes into Presenter View solves this problem.
- **Check that your images work when they're projected, not just on your computer screen.** If necessary, use a graphics package (my favourites are Pixelmator, followed by GIMP) to make the contrast of your images a little exaggerated – projectors often 'flatten' images. If you need to, it's often useful to explore the colour balance of the images too, as projectors won't always show the same balance of red, green and blue, etc. as your computer screen will.

## Source

Kustritz, M. V. R. (2014), 'Effect of Differing PowerPoint Slide Design on Multiple-Choice Test Scores for Assessment of Knowledge and Retention in a Theriogenology Course', *Journal of Veterinary Medical Education*, Vol. 41 No. 3 pp 311–17

## See also

Chapter 1 – There's more on the order in which you should provide information in: **First things first**

Chapter 13 – Giving people an indication of what to look for before they see it can be taken further and applied to people too – in the way they are introduced: **Being who you are**

Chapter 17 – Diagrams and graphics in your slides are looked at in: **The vexed picture question**

## Further reading

The concept of 'Presentation Zen' takes the idea of images (only) on slides to a whole new level. The man who originated the idea (Garr Reynolds) has put some before-and-after comparisons online at http://www.slideshare.net/garr/sample-slides-by-garr-reynolds

Even Forbes has got in on the act: http://www.forbes.com/sites/carminegallo/2012/09/12/powerpoint-the-extreme-makeover-edition-before-and-after-slides/

# 7 STAND UP! STAND UP!

*Does the way you stand when you're presenting matter?*

Amy Cuddy is a social psychologist with an interesting back story. Essentially, she had a head injury in her childhood which might well have ended things before they began. Nowadays, however, she's reached the dizzying heights of being a professor at Harvard Business School. She's nobody's fool!

If you get a chance to watch her make presentations (such as on the TED website – www.ted.com), you should grab a cup of tea and clear yourself a little time. I promise you'll find it worthwhile.

Back in 2010 she wrote a report that was published by the Association for Psychological Science. You can find it online if you want to fight your way through the whole thing.

To be honest, though, all you need to know is that by making some relatively easy changes in how you stand, you can have a significant impact upon how 'powerful' you are perceived to be by your audience. It can change your perception as well as your audience's too: Cuddy's research identified changes in the hormones of the presenter that relate to feeling confident and powerful.

Professor Cuddy built upon quite a bit of research that had found (unsurprisingly!) things like:

- winning a competition increases your testosterone level; losing a competition decreases it
- powerful individuals tend to be more happy to take risks
- low-power groups tend to have more stress-related illnesses, and this can be (in part) linked to chronically raised levels of a hormone called cortisol.

No surprises there, but Cuddy goes on. Previous research is pretty clear that 'power' results in displays of power. Just like me, I'm sure you've seen people who feel powerful and important standing or strutting around in certain ways that makes it obvious to everyone how they feel. Conversely, there's also research that things like hunched postures can make people feel more depressed. What there wasn't, until Professor Cuddy did her research, was the work that formally completes the cycle.

She turned the situation around to ask: does standing in 'dominant' or positive postures make the person doing so *feel* more powerful and dominant, even though they don't necessarily start off feeling that way?

Cuddy took 42 people and split them into two groups, randomly. They were then wired up to various bits of scientific instrumentation...

... before being fibbed to by the researchers about the nature of the research.

Participants were then 'posed' by the experimenter into what were thought to be high-power poses or low-power poses. The poses themselves were taken from a pretty comprehensive review of the existing research, and they were checked against the responses of observers when they saw the postures. Sure enough, people agreed with the literature that a man leaning back, with his feet crossed on the desk and his hands clasped behind his head was a 'high-power' poser. Standing with your head tilted downwards was a 'low-power' pose.

Why fib to participants? So that there was less chance of the research being messed up by people acting up to their expectations of the results. If people know they're in group X, they often start to act in way X. For example, people who believe they are drinking alcohol can start to act drunk, even if they're being given non-alcoholic versions of their drinks.

It seems okay to label it a 'white lie' to tell people that the experiments were about the process of collecting data from electrodes above and below the heart.

It's certainly whiter than many of the things I've said over the years!

After the posing came the measurements – and the all-important results.

People self-reported on a scale of one to four how powerful they felt – you can see now why it's important to fib to participants – so that they're not encouraged to change their responses. How likely people were to take risks was measured by checking their responses during a bit of gambling. Hormones were measured from saliva samples and compared to the levels taken before the posing.

By the way, the risk-taking measurement wasn't all that high-powered. It hardly reached the standards of James Bond in *Casino Royale*. Instead, participants were given US$2 and were given the choice of keeping it or trying to double it up on a 50:50 roll of the dice. No one was going to get rich quick on the back of the research, but that's not the point. What matters is comparing people from the two different groups, not the amount of money involved.

The results were unequivocal. People who had been posed (by other people don't forget; they'd not posed themselves) in high-power poses had significantly increased levels of testosterone compared to their pre-test levels. There was an even clearer drop in cortisol levels. (It's simplistic, but think of testosterone as an assertiveness/dominance hormone and cortisol as a stress/non-dominance hormone.) If you're interested in the science of it, there was much less than a 5 per cent chance of their results being randomly arrived at.

And when it came to the gambling... people in the high-power group took the 50:50 risk (rather than safely keeping hold of their cash) well over 80 per cent of the time, whereas only 60 per cent of the low-power group did so.

Finally, remember the self-reported feeling of power, measured on a scale up to four? There was a very clear statistical difference between the two groups, with the high-power posers feeling more powerful.

The implication for presenters is that how we stand can have a very marked influence on how we feel and how we act. By simply making sure we stand in 'powerful poses' we can deal with performance nerves and be prepared to take more (small) risks on stage, avoiding the boring, playing-it-safe demeanour of less-confident presenters.

It's always hard to design this kind of experiment and I'm sure you could see a lot of things that can possibly explain the results other than the nature of the posers at this point. If you're like me, the obvious weakness that springs to mind is that the poses might have been different in terms of how hard they were to maintain. High-power poses might have used more muscles, therefore pumping up the testosterone levels like a gym workout can, for example. Or it might have taken more contact between the researcher and the participant to put someone in a low-power pose and it was *that* process that made the difference rather than the pose itself. (By the way, scientists often refer to this problem – that the process of measuring something changes it – as the Hawthorne effect and it's a real pain for behavioural scientists of all kinds.)

Cuddy and co. tested for that in a series of subsequent investigations and found no problems.

In other words, it pretty clearly looks that just two, one-minute poses in different postures can actually make you feel more powerful. Pretty cool, huh?

Now obviously I'm not suggesting you strut around all day with your chest puffed up like a bantam, trying to do the presenter equivalent of a peacock spreading its tail feathers or a baboon baring its teeth, but there are a few ways a presenter can use this research with integrity. Professor Cuddy herself has said publicly, for example: 'Don't fake it till you make it. Fake it till you become it.'

As a side note, I personally find it useful to put instructions to myself about things like power poses into my delivery notes. Otherwise, the sad irony of the situation is that at the very moment when you most need to feel confident you're under the most pressure and you'll forget to apply this tool. But that's just me – your brain might work differently from mine!

And what do power poses look like? Well the most obvious one is generally referred to as the Wonder Woman pose, with your feet apart and your hands on your hips.

## So what are the big takeaways here?

- **Before you go on stage, power pose!** You might look like a bit of an idiot, of course, so it might be worthwhile finding somewhere private before you do. Try going to the bathroom, for example, and getting a minute or two to yourself. Most speakers have a warm-up routine, so why not simply try adding a minute or two of power posing to your regular routine?
- **Make a pattern of trying out high-power poses.** No one is suggesting you swagger around the office because you'll just look daft (though I've seen some people try, with various levels of success) – but what you might like to think about is taking a minute or two, here and there in your day, to do the positive stuff and let it all build up gradually.
- **At a couple of key points in your presentation, make sure you're using high-power poses.** This isn't just to look good, don't forget, it's also to make you feel more confident and powerful. An example might be at the start of your recommendations; or the point when you tell your boss what you think (s)he should be doing differently; when you get to the point where you reveal that the solution to the problem is that you should get a pay rise; or just about any point when you expect there to be a bit of resistance or scepticism to your message.

## Source

Carney, D. R., Cuddy, A. J. C. & Yap, A. J. (2010), Power Posing: Brief Nonverbal Displays Affect Neuroendocrine Levels and Risk Tolerance', *Psychological Science*
http://www.people.hbs.edu/acuddy/in%20press,%20carney,%20cuddy,%20&%20yap,%20psych%20science.pdf

## See also

Chapter 18 – For a very specific exercise to help with performance nerves, try **Fit to talk?**

Chapters 27 and 36 – There are other ways to handle your nerves: try **Fashionable fear** and **Minding what you say**

## Further reading

Join the other 26 million plus people who've watched Amy Cuddy talk about this directly on the TED website: http://www.ted.com/talks/amy_cuddy_your_body_language_shapes_who_you_are?language=en

**BEING SUBTLE**

*How much effect does your choice of words have?*

Presentations tend to use a lot of simplification – if they don't they risk being seriously boring, pointless and too long: after all, if you don't find some way of abbreviating the work you've done then the people in your audience might as well have done that work for themselves. Come to think of it, pretty much every communication uses simplification, for the sake of speed and convenience: we tend to give people only enough information to be getting on with. My (lovely) wife might ask me to buy something on the way home from the gym and she might mention it's for us to cook for tea, but she will stop short of listing all the other ingredients that we've already got at home, ready to be used.

One very common way of getting complicated ideas over to your audience very quickly is to use metaphors, and some work by Thibodeau and Boroditsky looked at exactly that – how effective are metaphors in influencing the way an audience thinks? They took as their starting point the level of crime in the United States (the US has only 5 per cent of the world's population but 25 per cent of its prison population) and looked at how different metaphors about crime affected the way participants in their experiments thought about crime – particularly in terms of what to do about it.

Before we go any further, it's important to note that their participants were students or people who use Amazon's Mechanical Turk system for finding and completing what to my mind are relatively trivial pieces of work: a quick look on the day I'm writing this suggests that, if I want to, I can find online pictures of Real Estate Agents for 4 cents in 7 minutes; spend an hour looking at the likely endings of an English sentence for 25 cents; or find URLs for movies for 6 cents, in 20 minutes. (Is it just me, or do some of those sound like the kinds of thing it's quicker to do yourself than to brief other people to do?) For this research work, the pay rate worked out at the equivalent of US$10/hour.

In the first experiment participants were given a short paragraph about crime in a fictional city of Addison. For one group, crime was described as a 'wild beast preying on' the city and in the other it was a 'virus infecting' the city. Everything else about the paragraph was the same and participants were asked to come up with options for what the city could do about crime and to underline the parts of the paragraph that were most important. A few people couldn't come up with any ideas at all and, overall, slightly more people came up with ideas in the 'enforcement' route (which Thibodeau and Boroditsky associated with the 'beast' metaphor) than with the 'reform' route (which they associated with the 'virus' metaphor). But the interesting thing is not so much the absolute numbers as the way those numbers were split up…

Participants given the 'crime-as-beast' metaphorical framing were more likely to suggest enforcement by quite some way. (Statistically there was a *p value* of less than 0.001, meaning that there is only one in a thousand probability of the results being due to chance.) What's just as interesting, however, is that when the most influential bits of the paragraph were looked at, only 3 per cent of the participants went for the metaphor. A whopping 97 per cent of people plumped for the statistics.

Personally, I would have been tempted to publish the results at that point, but Thibodeau and Boroditsky were more thorough and carried out several more experiments. For example, in the original experiment the metaphors were blatant but in a follow up, things were more subtle – so subtle in fact that there was only one word difference between the two alternatives: crime was a beast or a virus. That's it, nothing else was different, and yet the results were pretty much as they had been before. In other words, using a single word is enough to set people off down a train of thought (see me using a metaphor there?) to the extent that it influences their thinking about solutions to the problem.

From a presenter's point of view, the way we can use this is significant. On the upside it means we have a tremendously powerful tool at our disposal to shape the whole way our audience members tend to think. We can frame their whole response to an issue simply by looking carefully at which metaphors we use to introduce or explain our topic.

On the downside, precisely because the effect is so potentially potent, we need to be very careful with how we use it. To use a contrived metaphor myself, this is a sharp knife and we can cut ourselves easily. It behoves us to think very carefully indeed about our use of words: on a personal note, I make a point of trying to use several different metaphors, very early on when I'm presenting because I don't want to set my audience off in too-fixed a mindset; nor do I want to limit their way of thinking about possible solutions to problems or ways forward, and so on.

Don't forget, we're likely to be locked into our own metaphors for understanding and thinking about things. Imagine the round-table, after-dinner conversations about crime and immigration in the UK when I tell you that my father-in-law has something of a military background and way of thinking, and that I spent my early research years looking at the possible viral causes of childhood cancer... Our experiences, and therefore our personal world view, are *completely* different.

Thibodeau and Boroditsky wanted to see if the effect of the metaphor went even further, and so they showed a new group of participants the same paragraph but this time without the beast/virus reference in it. Instead, they simply showed those words to people first, and asked them to think of a metaphor for whichever of the two words they'd been shown. The idea was to 'prime' people to think in a certain way before they read the paragraph. This time there weren't any differences in how people responded to what they read. In other words, it appears that the presence of the metaphor is the trigger, not the mere idea of it.

That makes a difference to presenters, of course. It means that to trigger a certain set of audience responses, you need to be overt in your use of metaphor – you can't just use associated ideas or a conceptual framework and expect it have an effect.

Finally, Thibodeau and Boroditsky wanted to look at this phenomenon in more detail and so instead of simply asking people for their ideas, they presented them with a list of four ideas and asked them to pick one. These ideas were balanced between a more enforcement-oriented approach and a reform-oriented one with the idea that people were picking an area of interest, so that they could subsequently make specific suggestions. You can probably guess the results: people were more likely to go for the enforcement-based options if they'd read the 'beast' metaphor by nearly two to one. Those are remarkably powerful figures that presenters can make use of. Not only are people more likely to come up with ideas and solutions of a certain type if they are sent down that route by a metaphor but they're more likely to want more information in that area as well. The implications for affecting your audience's interests, suggestions and responses are both easy to see and potentially very powerful.

The question remains, however, about how the metaphor affects people's reasoning. Does it simply affect the types of outcomes (interests, ideas) or does it go further and actually affect people's very understanding? Thibodeau and Boroditsky argued that if metaphor affects understanding, it would have a bigger effect at the end of their paragraph than at the beginning – the logic being that if the metaphor is given at the end of the paragraph we might expect it to have a stronger effect, as it is fresher in people's minds, perhaps simply acting as a trigger for a pre-packaged set of responses.

Here, for the first time, we're in for a bit of a surprise. Now that the metaphor appeared at the end of the descriptive paragraph it had no effect. None. Nothing. We might have expected it to be more effective, because it's closer to the questions, so to speak, but instead it appears that putting the metaphor early in the description changes the way people assimilate and infer from the information that is presented subsequently.

As a presenter, this means you now know when to deploy this tool – as early as you can! If you get the metaphor in your audience's minds, they'll be inclined to interpret what you say in the light of that metaphor.

Again, though, I suggest you're careful how you use this. Once you're off down a particular metaphorical route it might be difficult to get your audience to change tack. I've found this to be a bit of a problem sometimes because while I've been working on a presentation I've had weeks or months to think about things using a variety of different metaphorical frameworks: your audience hasn't had that luxury and you're asking an awful lot of them to ask them to change tack in the middle of things.

A personal note here… be careful with your metaphors. My experience is that people who think in a very literal way or people who are challenged by the message of your presentation might challenge the validity of the metaphor itself, rather than concentrating on what you're really talking about.

As an interesting piece of follow-up work, Thibodeau and Boroditsky looked further into all of this with some interesting results: perhaps the most important of these is that the influence of the metaphor existed even when people couldn't remember the metaphor itself, which means, as presenters, we have an even more serious moral obligation to be careful about what we say and how we say it… but it also means the metaphor tool is potentially even more powerful.

## So what are the big takeaways here?

- Use a very carefully chosen metaphor to help your audience understand what you're talking about: you can get a lot of implicit meaning in one short sentence that way.
- Use your metaphor early and be sure you either stick to it all the way through (in which case it needs to be a very good metaphor) or at the very least you're clear and explicit when you start to use a different one.
- Consider using images as the basis for your metaphor – it might save you time and effort.

## Sources

Thibodeau, P. H. & Boroditsky, L. (2011), 'Metaphors We Think With: The Role of Metaphor in Reasoning', *PLOS ONE*, Vol. 6 Issue 2

Thibodeau, P. H. & Boroditsky, L. (2013), 'Natural Language Metaphors Covertly Influence Reasoning', *PLOS ONE*, Vol. 8 Issue 1

## See also

Chapter 16 – Metaphors get used a lot in stories – or even form stories of their own. See **Story time**

Chapters 20-22 – Professor Cialdini has a lot to say about influencing your audience. See **Power of persuasion** and the two follow-up chapters

Chapter 23 – Out of pure interest, see **The Lucifer Effect**, with its connection to crime

Chapter 35 – What's said and not said, seen and not seen is discussed more in **Blindness isn't in the eyes**

## Further reading

For a discussion of the different ways different types of people will tend to regard metaphors, try looking at the differences between people with a Sensing preference and those with an Intuitive preference in the famous Myers-Briggs Type Indicator. There are (literally) millions of places to read about this online but you can start at http://www.myersbriggs.org/my-mbti-personality-type/mbti-basics/sensing-or-intuition.htm

If you want to further explore how metaphors work, you should spend time at the always-wonderful TED website, see http://www.ted.com/talks/james_geary_metaphorically_speaking. It's a wonderful presentation – take your time with it and go over it twice (at least!).

**DIAGRAM DESIGN**

*Does the way you show figures have an impact?*

A picture's worth a thousand words, right? Usually. A lot of presentations show 'figures'. I'm using the word to mean a labelled graphic, not just a set of numbers. Graphs would count, as well as technical diagrams, but not photographs obviously. At this point it is worth mentioning two ideas to do with graphics: the Duck and the Golden Duck.

A 'duck' is a graphic that contains no information, or at least no information that's not better presented another way – such as a list. A 'golden duck' is something that does the same thing but in such a gloriously pretentious way it draws attention to itself. As an example: you've got a group of people, 48 per cent of whom are male? I think we can figure out for ourselves that 52 per cent are female. We don't need a pie chart to illustrate it ('duck') and particularly not a three dimensional pie chart with bells and whistles ('golden duck'). Got it? Good!

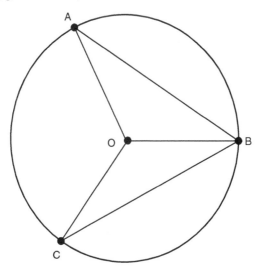

**Figure 9.1**

The labelled circle figure is typical of what I'm thinking about. Although I've not included them here, there are obviously going to be several statements associated with the figure, such as 'OB = OA = OC' and so on. If these are written down even slightly away from the figure, it can mean that anyone who's trying to work on the problem has to hold the figure in their head and read the information at the same time – in other words, they need to do more brain work.

You'll know exactly what I mean if you've ever had to read complicated assembly instructions when the list of things you had to do were on a different page to the image of how to do it.

As you might expect, that's not a random figure I've invented. It's copied from some nice work (with a title that tells you everything about the paper) called 'Reducing Cognitive Load by Mixing Auditory and Visual Presentation Modes'.

The idea is simple – groups of school students were given a set of maths problems, with the information presented in different ways, and how quickly (and accurately) they solved the problems was compared. As you can guess from the title, Mousavi and his colleagues were investigating whether something called the 'split attention' effect reduced (or possibly increased) people's ability to think clearly and quickly.

It's a problem with wider implications than just for education and presentations. For example, back in 2005 there was research interest in the way that splitting drivers' attention between the road and

One particularly famous study, called the 'infomania' study, was carried out in 2005 by Dr Glenn Wilson, but he didn't publish the results himself until some years later, as a partial result of the misinformation floating around which suggested the research had compared information overload with the effects of taking marijuana.

The real research found, simply, that when a (very small) sample of people were IQ tested in quiet conditions and again when there were lots of distractions, the latter conditions revealed a drop in IQ. And before you ask, yes, the drop-off was more for men than women, suggesting there really might be something in the idea that men can't multi-task as well as women.

different kinds of roadside advertisements might result in more accidents – particularly on bends, where, presumably, the driver needs to pay more attention to the road. And in business there's *always* interest in increasing productivity! Essentially, the idea is that the split attention effect causes a kind of information overload in people, so that they can't concentrate as easily on what is supposed to be the focus of their attention.

Back with the Mousavi maths research, the students were split into three balanced groups, known as the 'simultaneous group', the 'visual-visual' group and the 'visual-auditory' group.

| | Simultaneous group | Visual-visual group | Visual-auditory group |
|---|---|---|---|
| This is what the group experienced... | This group was given worked examples and as part of that they were given the associated figure and statements visually. At the same time they were given the statements played from a recording. What this means is that these people got the information twice, in different ways, at the same time. | This group was given the same information, but didn't receive the information orally – they weren't played the recording. They only had the visual information to go on. | This group got the recorded information, but they weren't given any written information other than the figure. |

(*Continued*)

|  | Simultaneous group | Visual-visual group | Visual-auditory group |
|---|---|---|---|
| … and this is what that means in terms of how they focused their concentration. | This group could ignore the auditory information and any effects of splitting their attention, or they could ignore the extra, written information, using the recording instead. | There was no choice for members of this group but to split their attention between the figure and the facts that went with it. | They had no choice about how to get that information, unlike the simultaneous group. |

Things were explained to students, they were given a time to get their brains around the problem and then they were given a number of problems to solve. Anyone who didn't get the correct answers inside of five minutes was given a score of 300 (the number of seconds in five minutes) but everyone else was given a score (in seconds) for how long it took to get the right answer – and the results were interesting.

Initially, the groups that received the audio recording took longer to get started (for the obvious reason that it took a while for the tape to play) but once they started they correctly answered the questions more quickly.

It looked as if there was something in the idea of reducing the demands on brain-work. On the other hand, it could be simply be because they took more time to get things sorted in their heads before they began to work. To check this out, Mousavi et al repeated the experiment, but this time making sure everyone got the same length of preparation time… and the results were more or less the same.

What does this mean for you as a presenter? Well there are a few fairly obvious things.

First, figures and diagrams should be labelled carefully (if they're labelled at all) so that your audience doesn't have to work so hard; keep labels on the figure, not off to the side or (worse still) on a different slide altogether. Second, it's perfectly possible to not label your slides, so long as you provide the necessary information yourself, telling your audience what they need to know (in fact, from other chapters, we know that this can mean people remember more of what you tell them).

Something I've found useful when I'm doing this kind of thing is to avoid putting labels on a diagram at all, and to give the audience a moment to get their individual 'mental bearings'. Then, as I talk about the figure, I fade in the labels on it one at a time. Of course, there's a lot more work to doing it like that, but for complicated diagrams the results are very much worth the effort. I have to admit, I was doing this even before I read the rest of the research here…

… and in another personal note, I have a confession: I spent a huge amount of my professional research life drawing maps – not just the kinds of maps most people use to help them to get from A to B, but maps designed to illustrate a specific point, such as the pattern of unemployment in the UK, or where immigrants from the EU were making a positive/negative impact upon the local economy, or (my personal favourite) maps intended to simply define what people mean by 'local'. In short, they could be pretty esoteric. However, it gave me more than 20 years' experience of labelling the most complicated form of diagram I've ever come across, and the appreciation that diagrams need to be designed with their end user in mind: imagine the map of the London Underground drawn as though it were physically accurate – you'd probably not be able to use it quite so easily as you can use the topologically twisted version we're all familiar with.

The British Cartographic Society freely admits there's no 'formula for making a well-designed map' but it does helpfully list a number of things to consider, which map nicely (if you'll forgive the pun) onto other forms of diagram as well.

- Clarity and legibility – starting with the obvious, because if people can't read your figure they can't understand your figure. There's a three-way balancing act between making sure your labels are next to what they refer to; that the overall thing looks good; and – importantly – that the labels are distinct and separate from each other. Labels that lie close to each other or to more than one feature of the figure are confusing.
- Hierarchy and structure – you can steer your audience to understanding what's important and what's less important by how you design your labels. It isn't just to help things look pretty, it makes the whole concept of your drawing much easier for people to understand.
- Colour and pattern – if you can, you should match your colours to things people expect, or at least recognize. Red for water would jar with people, for example. It's also important to consider that at least some of your audience is likely to be colour blind and won't necessarily see the same colours as you do.
- Visual contrast – the brain can only differentiate a surprisingly limited range of things like colours arranged in a spectrum, or the sizes of circles, so consider using two colours to show something or two shapes. Instead of red-through-to-white, for example, consider red-through-to-blue; and instead of large circles to small, consider large circles through to small triangles.

My personal experience is that it can take me 30 seconds to draw a diagram for my slides, but another 30 minutes to get it *right*. But it's always been worth the effort.

## So what are the big takeaways here?

- **Keep your labels for diagrams and figures clear and integrate them into the image,** not out to the side.
- **Consider describing your diagram, figures and so on, rather than just relying on people reading what's on the screen –** or better yet, providing different (supporting and relevant) information verbally.
- **Take into account the design advice for complicated figures such as maps and get your labelling to convey additional information that your audience will find useful,** such as how

important an object is or how it relates to other objects, rather than 'just being' a label. The figure itself should be clear enough not to need much by way of explanatory labels: if it isn't, think about redesigning it!

## Sources

Mousavi, S. Y., Low, R. & Sweller, J. (1995), 'Reducing Cognitive Load by Mixing Auditory and Visual Presentation Modes', *Journal of Educational Psychology*, Vol. 87 No.2 pp 319–34

Crundall, D., Van Loon, E. & Underwood, G. (2006), 'Attraction and distraction of attention with roadside advertisements', *Accident Analysis and Prevention*, Vol. 38 Issue 4 pp 671–7

*Cartography – an introduction*, The British Cartographic Society, London

## See also

Chapter 3 – It takes a bit of wrapping your head around, but the ideas of **Clarity is king** don't just apply to text and fonts – they apply to images and graphics too.

Chapters 17 and 19 – There's more on using images in **The vexed picture question** and **Doctors know best**

## Further reading

I'm not suggesting you need to go this far, but if you're interested in seeing how far you can take different forms of visualization, diagrams and graphics, you could do well to look at the work of Professor Danny Dorling. Danny's now a professor of geography at Oxford (and in the spirit of full disclosure you should know we started our research careers together). For a start, have a look at his work on 'cartograms': http://www.dannydorling.org/books/visualisation/Slideshow.html

(Don't forget Harry Beck's world-famous London Underground Map as an example of how very complicated data can be visually presented.)

Perhaps the doyen of visualizers for 'hardcore' data is Edward Tufte, who is responsible for the famous phrase 'PowerPoint® is evil'. You can find his books at http://www.edwardtufte.com

# 10 SAYING HELLO AT THE DOOR

*Does how you greet your audience make a difference?*

We all know that handshakes are important, right? Every bit of writing about etiquette and making a good impression talks about having a good handshake. But exactly how valid and reliable is this advice? After all, I've read some pretty flaky stuff online.

In 2000 researchers at the University of Alabama were looking at pretty much the same questions. In fact, there's a lot of research from before that, but a fair bit of it is as limp as many handshakes themselves. Chaplin et al spent considerable time and effort in looking at how much we judge a person's personality by their handshake and (less importantly from the point of view of making presentations in a way) how accurate those assessments were.

For all kinds of reasons, which I think are probably obvious to you, it's hard to assess handshakes – for example, a handshake is pretty much only going to be assessed, subjectively, by the person who's receiving the shake. So how do you standardize for different handshake receivers? Suffice to say that Chaplin et al's approach was a lot better than much that preceded it.

Mind you, that wouldn't be difficult. For example, less than a decade earlier, one piece of research examined handshakes of nearly 30 people who were in-patients at a psychiatric hospital. No matter how good the research might be, it's hard to see how you can generalize from that particular sample.

So what did Chaplin and his colleagues do? Well for starters, they sorted out eight things to assess, based upon a review of the literature: they decided to record dryness, temperature, texture, strength, vigour, how complete the grip was (a pet hate of mine is the fingers-only half-shake!), duration and, finally, eye contact during the handshake.

On top of this, they asked their handshake-raters to make estimates of subjects' (people participating in the experiments and being experimented upon) scores on the big five personality traits of extroversion, agreeableness, neuroticism, openness to experience and conscientiousness. And the people whose handshakes were measured were also measured, objectively – first by using the same big five variables, and then by adding measures of emotional expressiveness, positive effect and negative effect.

That's a lot of data, potentially.

The people who were the subjects of the experiment (I'll call them testees) were given a battery of personality tests designed to objectively evaluate the same eight measures (the big five plus the last three ideas).

Chaplin and the team also did what they could to standardize for the vagaries of different researchers giving different scores. First, their 'raters' were given a month of training in how to give responsive handshakes, so that they didn't lead things. The details of how they did this are as boring as they are comprehensive, so I'll spare you. All you need to know is that there was a reasonably strong correlation between the opinions of the different testers for each of the things to be recorded.

They also contrived a very complicated scenario for testing handshakes so that:

- the people who were being tested didn't realize it was their handshakes that were under scrutiny
- the people tested were tested several times by each tester
- there was a number of different testers for each testee, so that comparisons of the testers could be made.

So what were the results of all this effort?

First, there was a striking amount of agreement between the testers about the eight measures of the handshakes. What's more, there was a strong correlation between many of the different measures – for example, the duration of the handshake and the score for eye contact had a correlation of 0.6 (1.0 is the maximum); and 'strength' and 'duration' correlated at 0.84. In fact, these correlations were so high that Chaplin's team decided to create a compound score of these eight measures, called the Firm Handshake Composite, rather than analyse the individual measures of the handshake individually.

After all that, is there a relationship between this Firm Handshake Composite and the personalities of the testees, as assessed by the oh-so-carefully-trained testers? Yes, in general terms. The relationships weren't particularly strong, but they were there. For example, 'shyness' and the Firm Handshake Composite were negatively related at –0.29 while 'neuroticism' scored –0.24 and 'openness' 0.20 and 'extroversion' 0.19.

> Oh, by the way, while it's not so important in this context, the evidence from this research is that your handshake is at least partially accurate as a measure of some elements of your personality – it relates positively to your extraversion and openness to experience, and negatively to your neuroticism and shyness. Just like you'd expect, in fact!

In short, the testers in this experiment felt they were making reasonable assessments of a considerable number of elements of the subject's personality. There were some interesting (and complicated) gender-related issues for one of the measures in particular, the psychological measure of 'open to experience', but the pattern was clear. Testers rated subjects more positively if they had a handshake which:

- was stronger
- was vigorous
- continued for a reasonably long time
- had a complete grip
- was associated with good eye-contact.

The implications for speakers is pretty clear. We're often given the advice to 'meet and greet' our audiences if we can – welcoming them as they arrive. And now we know how our handshake should be, to do this to best effect.

Andrew Bayliss and Steven Tipper, from the University of Wales, took the eye contact thing a bit further in a fun little piece of research. They carried out a rather innovative and elegant experiment in which participants were shown the faces (on a computer screen) of people who looked, or didn't, in the direction of a variety of household objects that then appeared. Some of these faces predicted correctly where the household object would appear all the time, some never and some in an equal split.

At the end of the process, the volunteers in the experiment were asked questions about which faces they trusted most and which had appeared most often. Significantly, those faces that correctly predicted where things would appear were clearly thought to be the most trustworthy and the faces that participants had a preference for. In other words, looking one way – and thus steering people's gaze in that direction too – before 'betraying' them by having an object appear in the 'wrong' place, makes people less trustful and less popular.

It also appears from Bayliss and Tipper's work that the face itself doesn't modify this effect – it happens for all types of faces!

Obviously, as presenters there's little opportunity for us to cue our audience's gaze in one direction and then either betray them or not, but it does rather give a nice indication of how much information people take in by looking at other people's eyes.

## So what are the big takeaways here?

- **Greet your audience, if you can, and if it's appropriate do it with a handshake that is firm and full.** Put some energy into it, use a fully engaged grip, and make eye contact as you shake.
- **Regardless of what I've just written, don't worry about the individual bits of your handshake** – the person you're shaking with won't analyse different aspects individually. Just concentrate on an open and positive first impression.
- **Use your eyes during your presentation.** Eye contact with your audience is important. If your natural instinct is to be shy and avoid the gaze of strangers, fight it. A useful trick, if

your audience is more than a few metres away from you, is to look at the bridge of their nose. They'll not be able to see that you're focusing in the 'wrong' place and you won't have to suffer their gaze directly.

## Sources

Chaplin, W. F., Phillips, J. B., Brown, J. D., Clanton, N. R. & Stein, J. L. (2000), 'Handshaking, Gender, Personality and First Impressions', *Journal of Personality and Social Psychology*, Vol. 79 No. 1 pp 110–17

Bayliss. A. P. & Tipper, S. P. (2006), 'Predictive Gaze Cues and Personality Judgments – Should eye trust you?', *Psychological Science*, Vol. 17 No. 6 pp 514–20

## See also

Chapter 13 – Even before you greet people they can start to form an opinion of you. See **Being who you are** for an exploration of being introduced and the expectations it brings

Chapter 31 – Between people's expectations and shaking hands come first impressions when people see you: **Being judged**

## Further reading

The Beckman Institute has a brief introduction to the effect of handshakes at: http://beckman.illinois.edu/news/2012/10/dolcoshandshake

As you might expect, MIT has something a bit more heavyweight, see: http://www.mitpressjournals.org/doi/pdf/10.1162/jocn_a_00295

Going one step further than just shaking hands, you could always salute! http://www.bbc.co.uk/news/blogs-magazine-monitor-30679406

*What can presenters learn from (good) teachers?*

I can kick a football. Compared to most guys of my age I'm pretty good, because I'm fit and have a reasonable sense of coordination. But being able to do that doesn't qualify me to run my national team, or even run my local Premiership team. (Unlike most taxi drivers I've spoken to recently.) And so it is with schools. Most people have been to school but that doesn't qualify them to teach or even to necessarily pass comment on teaching.

The fact is that experiencing something doesn't always qualify us to know what it is we've experienced authoritatively. On a personal note, I take it as a great compliment when people approach me to ask how to become a professional speaker or trainer 'because it looks easy'. What they mean, of course, is that it looks like an easy way to earn money. As a choreographer friend once said to some ballet dancers who complained that the audience didn't understand their sacrifices to become dancers: 'If it looks like you're working hard, you're not working hard enough.' Brutal but brilliant.

Let's look at a report to the Sutton Trust from the Centre for Evaluation & Monitoring at Durham University. In many ways it's a withering, but beautifully written, examination of so many of the things that so many of us take for granted and think make for good teaching. Okay, so making presentations isn't teaching, but many of the outcomes are the same. Both teachers and presenters are passing on information in the expectation that people in their audience will change their beliefs or behaviours.

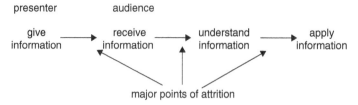

**Figure 11.1**

In other words, both school classes and presentation audiences are supposed to change their behaviour as a result of being given information. I think teachers have the advantage over presenters here, because they (generally) have an ongoing, better relationship with the people they're standing in front of than presenters do. Therefore, for presenters it makes it all the more important to make sure that the major points of attrition are reduced as far as possible to minor points of attrition. And the first of these (giving and receiving information) is the one most in the gift of the presenter.

Robert Coe and his colleagues (who wrote the Sutton Trust Report) have done a thorough job of looking at all the evidence for teaching – and in doing so have shot down quite a few myths that have crept into the general 'received' wisdom. Praising lavishly, for example, might make people feel good and is no doubt intended to encourage people, but the research found that all too often it can reinforce low expectations (as people get praised for poor work). A few of these myths have particular relevance to trainers:

- **Myth:** allow learners to discover key ideas for themselves – it's great news for presenters that this is a myth: it means there's some point in standing at the front of the stage and telling people things. We'd be rather stuck if it turned out that it's best to always let people learn for themselves!
- **Myth:** present information in people's preferred learning style – there's a whole chapter on this later in the book (Chapter 33 – Learning styles).
- **Myth:** ensure learners are always active rather than listening passively if you want them to remember – more good news for presenters! Essentially things like the learning pyramid (see below) are works of fiction, not of science.

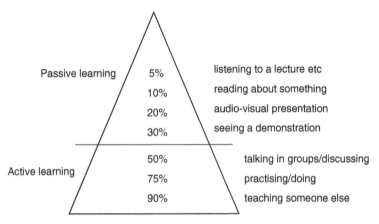

**Figure 11.2**

In terms of moving away from what doesn't work towards what does, there's a lovely straightforward list. It's so clear it's tempting simply just to quote the page of the report, but I'll resist the urge to be lazy!

The evidence that Coe and his colleagues cite tells us:

- **Variation:** don't stick to one style or one form of task. Chopping and changing (rather than being predictable) improves how much information is retained later – but might make your presentation rather unpopular in the short term because it makes your audience work harder.
- **Revision:** when you return to topics, make sure enough time has elapsed for people to have forgotten things just a bit – that is, for the items not to be at the forefront of their minds. If you use the same amount of time for revision and returning to topics (but don't do it in one big block) people remember more, precisely because they have to work harder to pull things back from memory. The more you spread it out, the better the chances that your audience will remember what you're telling them.
- **Cutting up:** my experience of presenting is that it's very often linked with training, so there's an additional point if your presentations fall into that category: interleaving presentation of information with other things 'leads to better long-term retention and transfer of skills'. Even if you're doing a pure

presentation (that is, not as part of any training) there are still opportunities to cut things up a bit. Mix up your presentation with other things, activities, and so on if you can.

As a presenter my instinct is always to put things into tidy boxes for my audiences, and they seem to appreciate that. But it turns out I'm not necessarily helping them by packing things so neatly! As Coe et al put it: 'One paradoxical finding is that some approaches that may appear to make learning harder in the short term and less satisfying for learners, actually result in better long-term retention.' In other words, you've got to decide what's more important to you as a presenter: short-term popularity or long-term learning for your audience?

## So what are the big takeaways here?

- **Decide if you want people to learn (rather than just listen to) what you're telling them.** If so, you should chop around a little more and make your audience work a little harder. Change your delivery style or medium when you can. For example, move from slides to flip charts when it's appropriate rather than sticking to one format all the time.
- **Refer back to things when they link.** Don't treat parts of your presentation as so complete that once they've been covered they are then essentially closed and can never to be looked at again.
- **Don't worry too much about keeping everyone 'active' all the time and don't try to double-guess the learning styles of the audience:** just use whatever 'mode' is appropriate for what you're explaining at the time.

## Source

Coe, R., Aloisi, C., Higgins, S. & Major, L. E., 'What makes great teaching? Review of the underpinning research', The Sutton Trust, October 2014

## See also

Chapter 4 – Jumping around topics and asking your audience to recall things is also handy if you want to build the 'illusion of truth', which is explored in **Repeating yourself**

Chapter 19 – Moving from how school students should be taught to what we can learn from how medical students should be taught, see **Doctors know best**

Chapter 33 – There's more about the (non-)existence of learning styles in the chapter called, predictably enough, **Learning styles**

## Further reading

Probably the first place to go to learn more about how to teach in your presentations is the TES website at https://www.tes.co.uk. Reading it is probably the law for teachers and if it isn't, it should be.

The Sutton Report that I've drawn on here is the work of the CEM centre at Durham University. CEM stands for the Centre for Evaluating & Monitoring and you can see what else they're doing here: http://www.cem.org/research

There's a lot of talk about how presenting and teaching are similar to stand-up comedy (to the point where the UK's Professional Speaking Association kicks off its national conferences with stand-up nights). This paper looks at whether there's real mileage in the analogy: creativityconference07.org/presented_papers/McCarron_Stand-Up.doc

# 12 OVERLOADED

*How do you avoid overloading your audience?*

Try to remember what it was like when you first learned to drive. If you're like me, and everyone else I know, you got to the point of being able to do the actual driving fairly quickly but if anyone started to talk to you while you were driving, you got tetchy. You might be more polite than me, but my early responses were to tell the speaker to 'shut up, I'm driving'. According to Cognitive Load Theory (CLT), this is because I'd reached the limits of what I could concentrate on (the driving) and that I knew it. If I was going to concentrate on the conversation I'd have to sacrifice some cognitive effort associated with the driving.

Wisely, I chose to concentrate on driving, not chatting.

Cognitive Load grows out of an understanding of how our brains process information and how the capacity for doing so is reached. Nowadays, proponents of CLT describe it as being made up of three components. One of which you are more-or-less stuck with, one you want to minimize and one you probably want to maximize.

## Intrinsic load

Intrinsic load is just that – it's intrinsically associated with whatever it is you're trying to get sorted out in your head. Some things have a higher intrinsic load than others, so (for example) advanced cryptography is harder to understand than a bread recipe and is said to have a higher intrinsic load. (I wonder what it says about my life that I've struggled with both, recently!) Different people will probably find different things have higher or lower intrinsic loads, I suspect, depending on their particular skills. It's this that you can't really change.

## Extraneous load

This is where you come in, as a presenter.

Extraneous load is the additional load you give your audience as a result of how you say things, how your slides are designed, and so on. In other words, extraneous cognitive load is the extra load done because of how things are taught, communicated or presented.

A bad explanation will have a high extraneous load and a good explanation will have a lower one. I can remember different teachers at school who managed to make something appear simple, while others made even the most simple of things overly complicated.

And if it's too complicated, we don't remember it. It's extraneous load that you want to minimize.

## Germane load

This is the fun one!

CLT has a core concept of the 'schema'. Think of a schema as shorthand for what you get when you've learned something and integrated it with the other things you know so it has become more or less automatic. Schemas can come in many forms, such as a skill (driving) or a pattern (recognizing a tree, despite the fact that all trees are different). In this sense, developing schemas is what learning is all about…

… And that means that audience members giving over a large part of their cognitive capacity to germane load is a good thing (all other things being equal, of course). It's this that you want to maximize.

To be blunt, if the combination of intrinsic load and extraneous load is more than the processing capacity of a person in your audience, that person isn't going to learn anything. As you can't (easily) reduce the intrinsic load, your only option is to look at how you can reduce the inevitable extraneous load.

As you read other chapters I'm sure you'll realize that this principle underlies a lot of the other chapters in this book, for example making sure that spoken and written content work together rather than simply duplicating each other, and once you get the idea that you're trying to minimize extraneous load common sense will let you figure out a lot of things for yourself.

An elegant example of this is some work of I-Jung Chen and Chi-Cheng Chang working in Taipei. Back in 2009 they noticed that when it comes to learning a foreign language, being anxious about that learning has a strong effect. It is postulated that Foreign Language Anxiety (FLA) is

> As an aside, it's interesting to note that there are only two big differences between experts and the rest of us. First, experts have large numbers of schemas at their disposal and second they have a high level of automation for skills – which is largely related to the breadth and depth of their schemas.
>
> That means that you, as an expert, will almost certainly find yourself thinking, saying and doing things that require almost no thought on your part but which can be very demanding on the part of an audience. You will have a schema in place for something they need to concentrate on and work out as they go along – which means it's very easy to lose people as your presentation continues.

a particular kind of anxiety related to a person's self-image, because working in a foreign language means they have to carry out tasks that they would perhaps find easy in their own language. Being 'bad' at something they *should* be 'good' at makes them feel anxious in potentially acute ways.

When you look at this in the context of CLT, the implications are clear. If learners are giving a proportion of their cognitive capacity to dealing with their feelings of anxiety they have commensurately fewer resources available to work on the task in hand. If the result is that too little capacity remains, they learn nothing.

This, unfortunately, would appear to be a case study mirroring many hundreds of hours of my life at school. Even now I come out in a cold sweat when required to speak a foreign language and I find it impossible to perform even the most otherwise trivial of tasks. When my French teacher asked me to count in French I found myself unable to count in English, let alone French!

In this research, the authors asked 88 students (who were not studying English) how much anxiety they had in relation to learning a foreign language. They were also asked to score themselves from one to seven for how much mental effort they put into a listening test. They were also asked to rate how difficult listening tests were in general. (The questions for this were all done in Mandarin Chinese.)

Unsurprisingly, students who had a higher level of anxiety tended to have a lower performance: students who worried about foreign languages did worse than other students who didn't. What's more, it turned out that this was despite working harder.

It's easy to forget that audiences in your presentations are often nervous, if not actually anxious about being there, so the obvious thing for you to do is to put your audience's minds at rest ('I won't be picking on anyone and making them answer questions in front of the rest of you!'). The implications of this work – and a lot of similar work – are much broader.

Anything that reduces your audience's ability to give you its cognitive load should be minimized. Quite a few of the other chapters deal with specific ways in which you can reduce the extraneous cognitive load, but here I want to concentrate on how you can do what you can to support the audience's cognitive capacity.

We've already seen that anxiety is a possible problem, so a bit of support and reassurance can go a long way, but what other possibilities are there?

## Physical issues

Being too cold or too hot can both distract audiences considerably. If they're trying to figure out how to stay warm they're not concentrating. Anyone who's trying to think about how to get out in a hurry at the end (to beat the traffic or whatever) is also unlikely to be giving you their full attention.

## Psychological issues

It's hard to concentrate if other things are on your mind. I know I've sometimes found it hard to get to the real core message of a presentation if I get hung up on the presenter's accent or a particularly irritating speech habit. More important, though, is the need to feel confident and that I can trust the presenter – and that's important in two ways; I need to trust you to not pick on me and I need to trust you to not mess up your facts. If I go away and act on something you've said, I need to be confident I'm not going to look stupid in front of my colleagues because you've got something wrong.

I can't begin to count the number of conversations I've had with people who needed some reassurance at the start of a presentation.

And what about anyone who's confused about where you are in the timetable. Or even what your name is? What about anyone who's shy or not sure they're supposed to be there, or worried about their boss being there or what they'll find when they return to their desk?

Something I've found useful over the years is a simple checklist of potential distractions. As soon as I'm set up with my slides (if I'm using them) I spend the rest of the time before my audience arrives going through it. Your checklist will be different from mine and I suggest you draw one up, but at the very least it should include:

- an emergency/safety check and reassurance
- a reassurance from you and then from all participants that what is said and asked will be confidential
- simple checks for temperature and noise
- a statement of how reliable your facts and figures are
- something that tells the audience how you'll deal with questions, so they know whether to ask them or keep them for the end
- a policy on handouts and notes, so people know whether to take notes, etc.

... and one more practice I've found very handy personally is to spend five minutes after I've tidied up at the end of a presentation to go over anything that happened, asking myself what could or should get added to that checklist.

## So what are the big takeaways here?

- **Do anything you can to put your audience's mind at rest about your content.** For example, simple statements about how you have checked the validity of what you're about to say, or who did the original research, can both be useful.
- **Deal with any 'housekeeping' issues up front and proactively:** people find it easier to concentrate if they know when the next break is, and can plan accordingly.
- **Before your audience arrives, sit in their seats and check that they will be as comfortable as you can make them.** Can they see easily, without having to move their heads? Is the room the ideal temperature for someone sitting down and not moving? Are distractions such as things happening through the windows minimized? Drawing the blinds can be a simple solution. It's frighteningly easy to overlook these details.

## Source

I-Jung Chen & Chi-Cheng Chang (2009), 'Cognitive Load Theory: An Empirical Study of Anxiety and Task Performance in Language Learning', *Electronic Journal of Research in Educational Psychology*, Vol. 7 No. 2 pp 729–46

## See also

Chapter 2 – Try also **You know that feeling when your head is full...**

Chapters 14-15 – See how much people can remember at once: **Why we can't remember long shopping lists easily (or is that just me?)** and **Chunking facts up**

## Further reading

Wikipedia is usually brilliant (but occasionally horribly wrong) because anyone can edit it. Assuming no one has messed it up recently the article on cognitive load is a handy quick read: http://en.wikipedia.org/wiki/Cognitive_load

Although it's a commercial organization, Mindtools often shares excellent resources, such as this article on cognitive load: http://www.mindtools.com/pages/article/cognitive-load-theory.htm

# 13 BEING WHO YOU ARE

*How can you influence your audience's expectations of you?*

In some ways it's hardly worth researching because we all know it's true: you're more likely to warm to a person or to think highly of them if they're introduced to you positively (by someone whose opinion you respect). Science being what it is, however, even things that fall into the 'everyone knows' category need to be tested. My personal, possibly cynical, experience of this as a researcher is that if my research validated other people's opinions then it was 'blindingly obvious' and I shouldn't have wasted public money and my time – on the other hand if I didn't validate other people's opinions the work was 'obviously wrong' and I needed to go back to the drawing board! My rantings aside, however, research into this area has a long history.

As early as 1950 students were being experimented on by fake professors. In a beautifully simple experiment Harold Kelley investigated the effect of introductions on three groups of third-year male students. The plan was simple: a previously unknown 'stimulus' person started a lecture by announcing that the regular lecturer was out of town and that there was an interest in how classes respond to different instructors, so they would be asked about the stand-in lecturer. In a move that might not get ethical approval today, students were then simply told that at the end of the lecture they were to fill in some forms about the guest lecturer and that to give them 'some idea of what he's like, we've had a person who knows him write up a little biographical note about him'. They were urged not to talk about the biographies that were handed out so that the lecturer didn't get wind of what was going on.

In reality, of course, the students were being lied to. Two different biographies were randomly distributed, identical apart from one thing – the guest lecturer was described as either 'rather cold' or 'very warm'. (Other details, common to the two bios, included the fact that he was a 26-year-old, married veteran and that he was industrious, critical, practical and determined.)

At the end of the lecture the students were reassured that their feedback was anonymous and that it wouldn't be used to get the lecturer into trouble. They then wrote a description of him in their own words and scored him on 15 scales for things such as:

| | | |
|---|---|---|
| Knows his stuff | vs | Doesn't know his stuff |
| Considerate of others | vs | Self-centred |
| Modest | vs | Proud |
| Generous | vs | Ungenerous |
| Important | vs | Insignificant |
| Will go far | vs | Will not get ahead |

Remember that there are three different groups of students involved in the research? In fact they responded so similarly that the results were pooled, and the average scores were then looked at. For every single one of the 15 measures, the scores were weighted towards the negative end of the spectrum for those people who'd been told the lecturer was cold, compared to those who had been told he was warm.

From a presenter's point of view, you can use this very simply (although your circumstances might prevent it being so easy in practice!). If you can, you should get someone to introduce you, or get a written introduction that biases the audience towards thinking you're the kind of person they want to listen to. For big presentations it's not difficult to find a compere to introduce you – though I recognize that if you're presenting to your colleagues at work you'll look like a bit of an idiot if you insist on a formal introduction. Nevertheless, you might be able to provide something in the background material that people read in an invitation email.

What's even more interesting was that these results didn't appear to be due to a vague, feel-good effect (called a 'halo effect') because the differences between the scores were very varied and not uniform, although always in the way I've described, and sometimes stronger than others. In his paper, Kelley suggests that the strength of the effect is directly related to how closely the measure is to the central concept of warm vs cold. For example, the biggest differences were noticed for things like social vs unsociable and considerate vs self-centred. It's easy to see how an adjective like warm/cold can influence those things more than measures such as intelligence or submissive vs dominant.

Incidentally, the results weren't affected by using a different stimulus person. It's dangerous to infer too much from such a small experiment, of course, but if this work can be generalized, it looks like you can be relatively relaxed about who does the introductions.

By the way, it's generally regarded as a good idea among professional speakers if the introduction finishes with your name. 'So, it gives me great, great pleasure to welcome our expert speaker for today, Dr Simon Raybould.'

Cue loud applause.

What this means for you as a presenter is that you can use this 'introduction effect' fairly precisely; it's not a blunt tool to crack all nuts. The introduction you need should be positive in those areas that are relevant to the things you're talking about. Personally, I know a lot of members of the Professional Speaking Association who write their own introductions. You might consider it a transparent trick, but as professional speakers they have found for themselves that Kelley's research works. And they don't have a one-size-fits-all introduction, but customize it for their intended audience.

More recently, Neil Widmeyer and John Loy took this idea a step further. They used a very similar set-up to Kelley's investigation, but performed a more rigorous statistical analysis, investigating three variables at once:

- warm vs cold
- a professor of physical education vs a professor of social psychology
- participant's gender (male vs female).

Those people who were primed to see the newcomer as warm rated him as a more effective teacher; more pleasant; more sociable; less irritable; less ruthless; more humorous; less formal; more humane. Whether the newcomer was a professor of physical education or social psychology had no effect, and neither did the sex of the participant. What that means to you as a presenter is that (other than the obvious feeling of confidence that the earlier research has been successfully replicated in different conditions, so you can trust it more) you don't need to worry about other things having an effect that undermines the impact of your carefully crafted introduction. Good news, indeed.

Of course, while it might not matter so much who introduces you, it will certainly matter how they do so. Just saying nice things might not be enough: it has to be the right nice things said in the right way. This was the very question addressed in a series of experiments by Richard Miller et al with schoolchildren in the United States.

Previous work had found quite a few things that increased the likelihood of successful persuasion in this kind of situation and the most important ones were:

- a high-credibility source
- a repeated message
- an explicitly stated conclusion.

The research was designed to maximize those three elements while looking at littering behaviour in the school and achievement in mathematics.

As a presenter you might not have as much control over everything as you'd like, but the three items in the list are something to aim for. Given the choice, I'd rather be introduced by a fellow expert who is known to my audience than by the person in charge of running the meeting, if they've just been brought in to do only that; and I'd rather my biography was printed in the running order of the day than just on a scrappy bit of dog-eared paper handed out while the audience was sitting down.

The experimenters made conscious attempts to manipulate the pupils in the school in one of two ways – in what I'm going to call 'attribution' and 'persuasion'. In the former, pupils were simply told things like they 'were tidy' and they already 'were good at mathematics' whereas the second group was simply exhorted to 'try harder' or told things like 'you should spend more time on maths'.

While you can't always control all the things manipulated by this research, the main points are pretty handy for a presenter. For both maths and tidiness, things improved, as you might expect if you think about your teachers at school constantly going on about something. However, what's important for presenters is that things improved considerably more if the teachers simply attributed abilities and behaviours to the pupils, rather than trying to persuade them. What's more, the effects lasted longer.

In other words, by simply telling people they were better at maths, they became better at maths. By telling them they were tidy people they became tidier people. I'm not sure if simply telling me I'm better looking would make me better looking, but imagine how you can use that when you're introduced. Simply by having a credible source tell your audience you're an expert, may mean you effectively become more of an expert in their eyes.

Perhaps more useful, in certain situations, is the idea that you can use this technique during your presentation to guide your audience towards certain behaviours and beliefs about themselves. Done crudely it's laughable – and I've certainly laughed out loud at some motivational gurus who get their audience to stand up and proclaim that they're winners, that they're going to get the life they deserve – but done well and with subtle flair it can certainly produce results.

## So what are the big takeaways here?

- **Get yourself introduced: don't just start talking.** And if you get yourself introduced by someone with a lot of credibility as far as the audience is concerned, so much the better.
- **Write your own introduction if necessary** and at the very least have it written in conjunction with you, so that you can customize it, emphasizing the things that you expect your audience needs to be primed for.
- **Make sure you're described as already 'being' something, rather than 'becoming' something** – an expert rather than a researcher, perhaps. Similarly, make sure your presentation is introduced as '*will be* a fascinating introduction to…' rather than letting the person who introduces you get away with saying '*should be* a fascinating introduction'.
- **As an added takeaway…** Remember too, that you can prime your audience to behave in certain ways – it's not just about you.

## Sources

Kelley, H. H. (1950), 'The Warm-Cold Variable in First Impressions of Persons', *Journal of Personality*, Vol. 18 Issue 4 pp 431–9

Widmeyer, W. N. & Loy, J. W. (1988), 'When you're hot, you're hot! Warm-cold effects in first impression of persons and teaching effectiveness', *Journal of Educational Psychology*, Vol. 80 No. 1 pp 118–21

Miller, R. L., Brickman, P. & Bolen, D. (1975), 'Attribution versus persuasion as a means for modifying behavior', *Journal of Personality and Social Psychology*, Vol. 31 No. 3

## See also

Chapter 6 – It's not just people who need introductions – so does data: **It's not what you say, it's the way that you say it**

Chapter 8 – How people think of things is very much framed by the descriptive context, too. See **Being subtle** for a discussion of metaphors

Chapters 10 and 31 – Other follow-ups are how presenters are greeted at the door and how they are first appraised. See **Saying hello at the door** and **Being judged**

Chapters 25 and 23 – For another look at how easily people can be influenced by other people's opinions see **Blaming the right people** and for a very depressing examination, see **The Lucifer Effect**

## Further reading

This is aimed well and truly at professional speakers (or at least would-be professional speakers) but the principles can also be applied to everyday life. Trust me on this: professional speakers are not real people – http://jeremynicholas.co.uk/2014/08/17/howtowriteanintroductionforyourtalk

If you're in any doubt about how effective a good introduction is, just try watching a new TV programme and see if what you expected from the opening sequence/credits gives you any expectations. If you're still not convinced, watch Thunderbirds! https://www.youtube.com/watch?v=D_mBUaPsX6o

For further stories on the effectiveness and importance of good introductions take a look at: *Yes! 50 Secrets From the Science of Persuasion* by Noah Goldstein, Robert Cialdini (he crops up a lot in this book!) and Steve Martin (Profile Books, London, 2007)

The book *Yes!* is a good, easy read, but if you want something snappier, try the 'Influence at work' blog, perhaps starting with http://www.influenceatwork.com/persuasion-the-third-leg

# 14 WHY WE CAN'T REMEMBER LONG SHOPPING LISTS EASILY (OR IS THAT JUST ME?)

*How much can your audience remember?*

Your brain is a wonderful thing. Some brains are more wonderful than others, of course, but overall, they're pretty amazing. As a result, people have been researching how they work for a long, long time. Way back in the depths of time (in terms of psychology as a science), George Miller was looking at how memory worked.

In 1956 while at Princeton University's Department of Psychology he published a paper in *Psychological Review* that looked at something called 'working memory'. It's now one of the most cited papers of all time. You can think of working memory as the amount of information you can cope with at any one time. When it gets overloaded you start to be unable to process things – a bit like a juggler taking more and more balls until it all gets a bit much and balls end up on the floor.

Miller's paper is big and complicated, but it started off looking at binary comparisons and gave rise to the idea of 'bits' of information. He uses height, but gender is an easier idea to work with, I think. People are (let's assume for simplicity) either male or female and we need just one extra 'bit' of information to know which they are. What that means is that with two bits of information we can handle four possible outcomes; with three bits, eight and with four bits of information, 16 outcomes.

| Using just two 'bits' of information... | Bit of information one (male vs female) | |
| --- | --- | --- |
| Bit of information: two (with glasses vs without glasses) | Outcome 1 – man without glasses | Outcome 2 – woman without glasses |
| | Outcome 3 – man with glasses | Outcome 4 – woman with glasses |

The simple table shows how that might work. You can see how quickly even binary options multiply to give us a lot of options for us to keep in our heads – which is ultimately what Miller was looking at. He was interested in what he called 'absolute judgement', which means he ignored things such as how fast someone can process bits of information and instead concentrated simply on how many bits they could handle at one time. For example, this can be done by asking people to identify different played musical notes, and counting how many times they get it right.

He comes to a rather depressing conclusion about how smart we are as a species.

For just one, two or three notes, people rarely get confused. That makes sense. With four different notes mistakes are still pretty unusual. That also makes sense. Then, rather suddenly, with five or more notes involved, mistakes are commonplace. What this seems to mean is that we can only handle a limited number of bits of information at a time, before things start to get out of hand.

Depressing, eh? Miller's paper goes on to look at how robust this finding is by talking about a range of things other than musical notes. He also reviews work on how salty something is, for example. It's important to remember that all of this is based upon looking at only one dimension at a time. For example, saltiness varies from 'not' to 'very' and musical notes (in this research) range in only one dimension, from 'low' to 'high'. When you start to look at things that vary with different dimensions – such as colours being light or dark vs bright or dull, perhaps – things get messier – but the long and short of it is that we can handle a few more possible outcomes.

Things interact so that, as Miller says, 'as we add more variables to the display, we increase the total capacity, but we decrease the accuracy for any particular variable. In other words, we can make relatively crude judgements of several things simultaneously'.

Miller suggests that we can only cope with around seven bits of information. I'd like to think I can remember more than that, of course, because I've got more than seven friends and they've got different names, but that's not what Miller was talking about. He was looking at how much information we can handle at once.

What he means is this – we can only discriminate a very limited amount of information at once, and adding variables to what we're looking at means we reach our maximum capacity very quickly: to compensate we tend to be less sensitive to variations on each dimension so the overall amount of information we're trying to handle is held down.

The final result of Miller's musings and observations – and of the subsequent musings of other people about Miller's work – is the so-called Miller's Law: people can handle seven pieces of information at a time, plus or minus two. (Don't forget, there are exceptions to every rule!)

Don't panic, stay with me, because I'll look at the bigger picture in a while, but for now, how you apply Miller's Law to your presentations should be pretty obvious and can be summed up like this: don't overload your audience with too many facts and figures at once. They can't cope and they'll start to make mistakes, getting confused between them. It's a bit like trying to watch a TV programme with so many characters that you lose track of who's who, particularly if they're similar to each other. If one twin is good and the other is evil, but there are too many people all together and one of the characters is wearing another one's clothing... well I just get confused.

I need tags or subtitles as characters come on the screen to remind me who they are. 'James – John's brother. He's the one who was by the river with his friend's wife two scenes ago but with her sister in the same place two episodes ago. He's also had plastic surgery (or at least that's what they pretended when they changed the actor) so you need to remember he was also the person who started the fire in the chip shop.'

Is it just me, or does that sound like an episode of *Hollyoaks*?

Your audience needs these tags as well. They can't keep too much information in their heads at once. Maybe it's just coincidence but ask yourself how many central characters there are in successful, long-running sitcoms or adventure series. There were six *Friends*; the Starship *Enterprise* had a crew of more than a thousand but we were only ever interested in seven or so; *Big Bang Theory* has about the same number of key characters. Don't get too hung up on that – there's no evidence behind it other than my tendency to watch too much TV.

Let me try to recover my credibility. I once read Stephen Hawking's *A Brief History of Time*. It's a great, great book but it contains so much information it's impossible to read and absorb at one go, especially as much of the information is challenging. I found myself understanding each and every page I read at

This doesn't mean you can't give your audience more than seven pieces of information, of course – it just means you can't expect them to hold much more than seven pieces at a time. You can give them more, but only if you give them time to digest things first.

The tricky part, of course, is that these bits of information are all new for your audience – but not for you. That means that no matter how hard you try, you're not going to be able to see things afresh. I suggest you get someone else to go over your presentation with you before you deliver it, just running through and looking for individual facts and figures. Keep a running total of what's likely to be in the audience's heads at any one time. Of course, using your friends this way might mean you lose them quickly, but at least you'll get a fresh perspective on your intended presentation.

the time I read it, but unable to remember what I'd read more than three pages later. I had to keep going back over material to remind myself what X meant, so that I could understand how it fitted with Y to give Z. The only reason I got through it was because I was stubborn (and on a bet).

## So what are the big takeaways here?

- **Don't give your audience long lists of things** – or at least don't do so if you expect them to be able to remember or compare them. Don't ask them to rank more than seven or so things. Stick to the limit of what people can process in the moment. Don't give example after example after example to prove your point – there's no point!
- **When you've got lots of information, there's no advantage in bombarding your audience with it.** You've got to drip-feed it. And then you've got to wait. You've got to wait until they're ready to move on.
- **Keep it simple.** Are you sure you need every single fact, figure or item of information you've included? Would a summary do? An average? A lot of presenters include stuff that's not necessary out of fear of missing something out and end up drowning their audience. When you've written your presentation, go back over it, looking at your facts, and see if you can cut them.
- **Be brutal – don't ask if you can cut it.** Let your default be to 'cut' and see if you can justify it. Remember that you've only got 7±2 to play with.

## Source

There's an online version of Miller's work at: www.musanim. com/miller1956. It's largely a review of previous work, crucially has his approval, and is written quite nicely.

## See also

Chapter 15 – Miller's work goes on! See **Chunking facts up**

Chapter 34 – Processing information as it's given to you, and ensuring you never have to work with more than seven items of information, can be helped by your audience taking notes. Try **Writing down your wisdom**

## Further reading

For something that's also beautifully written, but harder to understand, try: Stephen Hawking's 1988 classic *A Brief History of Time*, originally published by Bantam Press.

# 15 CHUNKING FACTS UP

*How do you get past the seven facts barrier?*

Miller's work (see the previous chapter) turned up a couple of other interesting bits and pieces for presenters – he didn't stop with just 7±2. Oh no, he went on. As well as this 'span of absolute judgement', Miller suggests that we also have a whole raft of other tools at our disposal. As he puts it: 'everyday experience teaches us that we can identify accurately any one of several hundred faces, any one of several thousand words, any one of several thousand objects, etc. The story certainly would not be complete if we stopped at this point.'

To prove the point, Miller goes on to review the research that observes that people can remember more digits in a row if they're paired up. The word Miller uses is 'chunking'. Bits of information are chunked together so that we can remember more. For example, one and three together can be thought of as 13, which is only one bit of information, not two. Obviously, therefore, the sensible way of remembering more stuff is to build a chunk with information in it, then nest those chunks into bigger chunks and so on.

Pretty obviously we can remember a lot more than just a list of seven things if those things are related, too; for example, most pieces of music are longer than seven notes. That's possible because the notes are related to each other in a pattern.

As an aside, it's a pretty cool trick to use a mnemonic to create an artificial pattern in what looks to the audience like random bits of information, and watch a full deck of 52 cards recited in the correct, but random, order. I'm not saying it's easy, but it's worth a standing ovation when the performer gets it right!

Maybe this analogy will help explain what I mean. Let me pretend I've got lots of friends for a moment, and that I need to remember how to get in touch with them all, what they look like, and so on. Excluding the area code, phone numbers in the UK tend to have seven digits, and yet I can remember a lot more than just one phone number. That's because I chunk the digits of the phone number up into one 'thing', put that thing in a box and label it 'phone number'. Then I put other information in other boxes, such as 'address' or 'looks' and put all those boxes inside another, bigger box and label that last box 'David'. Each of my friends is a box with smaller boxes inside it. I must admit, this model has intuitive appeal to me.

Come to that, just look at how we remember the actual phone numbers when we have to dial them. We don't try to remember the full set of digits in one go. Instead we group them together and don't try to recall the digits in the second group until we've recited the digits in the first. Try it. People in London, for example, seem to recite a number like this: area code – three digits – four digits. My office number isn't a list of 11 digits when I say it out loud. When I try to use it, my number comes to mind in groups – xxxx-yyy-zzzz.

Miller's jargon for this process is 'recoding'.

Alongside 'recoding' Miller says we also, essentially, paraphrase. What he means here is that we create a description of what it is we're trying to remember and that description is what goes to our memories, not the actual thing itself. We don't remember all the facts about a television; we remember the *concept* of 'television' and when we need to recall a television we bring to mind the *concept* and rebuild the details from memory, possibly unpacking only the 'boxes' we need at the time. That means we don't have to worry ourselves about remembering what channels are in what order if what we're trying to do is remember how to adjust the colour settings.

Perhaps it's easier to remember things this way, because now we're trying to remember the concept *expressed in our terms*, rather than the details.

Let's apply this a bit. I'll bet the cash you've paid for this book as a donation to your favourite charity that you've used a spreadsheet program at some point in your life. Microsoft's Excel is the most popular but there's also Google Docs, Apple's Numbers or OpenOffice's version. It doesn't matter what software you use, the point is that you probably don't know how it works. No seriously... knowing how to use it is not the same as knowing how it works. You probably know how to drive a car but do you really, really know how it works?

I'll bet you've not only used the software but you've used it to sort a column of numbers, right? Do you know the details of the algorithm Microsoft uses to do the sorting? Chances are, unless you're a serious hardcore coding geek, you won't have a clue. Nor will you care. It's a metaphorical sealed black box. You can open it up and see the super-fine coding inside if you want but if you don't understand it, that's fine too. You just close the box and remind yourself that what really matters is this:

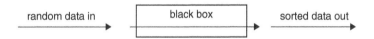

Each section of your presentation can work the same way, with data chunked up into sections or chapters or modules or units – call them whatever you like! – and each of these are more or less self-contained.

If you're not convinced, look at how you follow a recipe in a book. First comes the list of ingredients (and good luck with remembering the list if there's more than $7\pm2$) then the method steps. You read and follow each individual step in turn. Once you've followed it, you forget it and move on to the next step. At the exact moment when you're following each step you understand everything you need to to follow the instructions. Then, just a couple of steps later, you've moved on and can't really remember the details of the previous steps – or at least not without a conscious effort. You might remember the steps, but not the contents of those steps (the details).

In your presentations, by all means use 7±2 facts inside a chunk, but then close the chunk and move on. You can go into detail inside a chunk (think of them as black boxes), then close it again. If people have understood what's inside the chunk, that's great. If not, all they need to know is what happens inside it, not how it works.

Perhaps this example will help. A lot of us will have used a spreadsheet, such as Microsoft's Excel, and we'll have sorted columns of data with it. But how many of us actually know how the sorting is done, in terms of the computer coding? Not many. And we don't need to. We can 'open the box' if someone explains it to us but we can then 'close the box' again when the explanation is over (or if we don't understand it!) and move on, effectively erasing the detailed information from the front of our minds.

It also helps if the chunks (or for that matter the information inside those chunks) are presented in an obvious pattern so that they are linked in a sensible, sequential way inside the audience's head, just like notes in a melody. Personally, I've found a very easy way of doing this is to see if you can link from one chunk to the next with an obvious question or link. 'Of course, all this stuff about X only makes sense if we can do Y, so let's have a look at how practical Y is.'

If you can't find an obvious linking sentence like that, it's a big hint that your presentation doesn't have a coherent structure and your audience will find it harder to follow and remember.

## So what are the big takeaways here?

- **Present your work in 'chunks'.** Close your chunks off before moving on.
- **Keep your chunks in a sensible, logical (and obvious) sequence.** The order of the chunks is one of your 7±2 items itself, so use it wisely.
- **Put breaks into your presentations where the audience can do their own chunking.** Black slides are an obvious way to do this, as they clearly signal the end of something that people can then chunk up for themselves. Another good option is to encourage people to have a brief conversation about whatever you just spoke about with their neighbour.

## Source

See the approved, online version of Miller's work at:
http://www.musanim.com/miller1956

## See also

Chapters 2 and 12 – Sometimes you and your audience can get overwhelmed by 'stuff' in other ways, too. See **You know that feeling when your head is full...** and **Overloaded**

Chapter 14 – For the first part of a look at Miller's work, see **Why we can't remember long shopping lists easily (or is that just me?)**

## Further reading

Sometimes the idea of 7±2 gets taken too far. This blog/rant in the usually excellent UXMYTHS blog gives some illustrations:
http://uxmyths.com/post/931925744/myth-23-choices-should-always-be-limited-to-seven

Don't forget that if your audience doesn't need to hold things in their heads, you can happily go for more than 7±2 items. The whole blog is worth exploring, as many of the principles for User Experience (hence the name of the blog) of websites can translate to slides with a little imagination.

If you want to increase your working memory to get past the 7±2 limits there are lots of websites designed to help you – some of them better than others – but before you get carried away, you should probably be aware that even if you can increase your working memory, it won't make you smarter: http://www.psychologicalscience.org/index.php/news/releases/brain-training-may-boost-working-memory-but-not-intelligence.html

# 16 STORY TIME

*Do narratives have a place in presentations?*

This could be a very short chapter. The answer is 'yes'. Mind you, if you believed the hype in 'leadership development' circles over the past five years or so, you'd think that stories were the only tool around... This is surprising if you consider the lack of research in the area (compared to other things, at least) but perhaps less surprising if you think of it in terms of people needing to find a market for themselves. Maybe I'm unduly cynical.

Cynicism and related emotions were the very subjects of one of the most powerful of pieces of research that does exist about the efficacy of stories. It even appears in the title of the research: 'Sympathy and callousness'.

Before they started their research, the researchers already knew a few things from previous work:

- when valuing things that are hard to pin down to a specific market value (things like life and happiness), people show less responsiveness to greater numbers than to larger proportions. What that means is that five out of ten gets a bigger response than fifty out of a hundred.

How responsive are we to stories? You only have to look at the news to be inundated with reports of bad things happening. Grabbing my news feed today I can find something big, bad and depressing on every continent of the world (except Antarctica, unless you count the background environmental stories). And yet some of these generate more reaction than others.

For some, the news story touches a nerve in the audience and the audience – us – responds. I'm old enough to remember the original Band Aid story of famine in Africa and like so many of my friends I stood watching the TV with tears pouring from my eyes – and yet both before and since then there have been famines

- people respond much more favourably to 'identifiable' need than to 'statistically defined' need. That is, people are more generous, for example, if they know about a specific victim rather than just knowing that there are lots and lots of victims. (In fact, there is some research to suggest that identification can increase feelings for negative reactions as well as positive ones.)

that haven't caught the public imagination in the same way. So what is it that makes the difference? Could it be in the way the story is presented to us?

As presenters this gives us something to think about. If we can, it looks very much as though we should find ways of making what we're saying personally identifiable to the audience: they need to make a personal, emotional connection if we're to increase the chances of them acting on what we say. It also means that we should express things in terms people can understand – the accepted explanation of people responding to proportions is that they're easier to understand than big, abstract numbers. It might sound horribly trite, but this implies you should think about analogies that translate what you're saying into the world your audience lives in.

Instead of just saying something like 'One hundred thousand deaths' consider saying 'One hundred thousand deaths, which is the same as one in every five people in the city of Sheffield'. Try to make it more relevant to your audience: people in Wales might not care so much about Sheffield as people who actually live there.

Moving on to the 'Sympathy and callousness' research...

Students were paid US$5 to complete a survey (the survey itself was an irrelevant device, just an excuse to pay the students) and they were then offered the chance to donate some of their new found wealth to Save the Children. Here's where the experimental bit begins. Some of the participants were given information about the work of the charity in terms of statistics and numbers; others were given the same information in the form of an identifiable story. Cross-cutting that, some were given an 'intervention', which told them about the tendency of people to give more when they identified with the victim.

The results were, perhaps, inevitable: people were more responsive (that is, they gave more money) when they had a story that allowed them to identify with the victim, compared to when they had statistical data only. However, when they were told about this tendency, the amount of response fell for those people given the story-based information down to the level for those people who were given the statistical information. As presenters this has implications for how we present information. If you want a big response, give your audience something they can identify with: if you want a smaller response, you should give them statistical information – or at least warn them not to trust their emotional responses!

The research takes this idea even further by simply priming some participants with quantitative questions, such as 'if an object travels at five feet per minute how far will it reach in 360 seconds?', and others with qualitative questions such as how they felt when they heard the word 'baby'. Even though the questions had nothing to do with the subsequent possible charity donation, they still had an effect: the first group responded less than the second – presumably because the first group was primed to think in an objective way and the second was primed to respond emotionally.

From a presenter's point of view this can have really serious implications in how we set our audiences up to respond to what we're saying. I've seen dozens of (even professional) speakers start their presentation with bold facts and figures (sadly expressed in absolute terms) designed to shock the audience into action, then give the audience examples of how they can react... and then be surprised and disappointed when the audience's response was lukewarm, at best.

If you want big reactions, don't dilute the effects of your stories and personal connections by setting your audience up to think logically, abstractly and in terms of statistics.

Of course, it's not just what you say, it's the way that you say it; and a story told in a halting, apologetic way might not have the same impact as one told with confidence. As you might expect, this is a fertile ground for researchers because of the social implications. I'm sure you won't be surprised, for example, to find that high-powered people have been found to use fewer conditional 'politeness' phrases when they make requests.

> Both speech and how you look at your audience is important. The rest of the chapter talks about your speech patterns, but just to illustrate how important it is to look at your audience…
>
> … researchers trying to develop a robot that can tell stories (you've got to ask what they were doing when they come up with this idea as a research project!) found that in a recall test about a story the robot had just told them, the research subjects did better when the robot looked at them more.

As a presenter, this suggests you should think carefully about how many times you say something in a conditional way, such as 'could I ask if you would just take a moment to…' or 'I wonder if I might have just a little of…' or 'is it possible to ask a favour?'.

Personally, it drives me nuts when *The X Factor* judges do this. They tell a terrible contestant: 'I'm going to have to say "no"', as though someone was pulling their strings. Who do you think is more authoritative? Judges who equivocate like that, or Simon Cowell, who tends to say 'it's a no from me'.

Meanwhile, back as far as 1978, research in the *Duke Law Journal* looked at the credibility of witnesses, based on their speech patterns. One of the beauties of this work, for me, is that it uses real data – they simply recorded all the cases in their local court over the summer, giving more than 150 hours of data. And in listening in, the researchers noted a pattern of witnesses who 'hedged' and those who didn't. (Hedging is adding things like 'you know' or 'I guess I do' after saying 'yes'.) With that distinction in mind, the researchers created recordings of 'powerful' and 'not powerful' testimonies, either with or without hedging, etc. Actors then recreated the testimony in front of groups of participants who were then, in turn, asked their opinions of the witnesses.

As presenters, the results are fascinating and how to apply them is obvious. In everything that was measured, including things that couldn't possibly be judged from the testimony such as intelligence, the 'powerful' speech patterns gave better results. Clearly the lesson for presenters is that we shouldn't equivocate in how we say things: clear, sharp, simple sentences are best (perhaps particularly in response to questions).

The Duke University researchers weren't finished here though. They went on to look at the differences between witnesses who gave an ongoing narrative (which didn't need many questions to make it clear) and compared it to witnesses who gave shorter, more obtuse statements – short paragraphs on the one hand, a series of sentences and questions on the other.

Questions and answers were less effective at giving people positive impressions than if the speaker used an uninterrupted narrative – or at least they were in the courtroom.

And finally, wringing every last bit of information they could out of the data, the researchers found that witnesses who 'tried too hard' to use overly correct grammar, posh words (and who consequently made mistakes or tied themselves in linguistic knots) were less trusted and thought to be less authoritative. The moral for presenters? Simply be yourself and don't try to speak in a way you'd not usually use. You're more trusted if you speak normally than if you try to speak 'properly', it seems.

## So what are the big takeaways here?

- **Use stories to create identifiable connections between your audience and the information you're delivering.**
- **Be careful about giving information in absolutes.** Unless it's translated into terms your audience can understand (such as by some kind of story that allows them to identify with it or making it personal), it's hard for them to take it in.

- **Don't equivocate or hedge (or be too parsimonious in) what you say.** People trust you more if your presentation flows, without lots of conditional phrases added in, and without the need for clarifying questions. But stick to your own style – don't try to be too 'proper'.

## Sources

Small, D. A., Loewenstein, G. & Slovic, P. (2007), 'Sympathy and callousness: The impact of deliberative thought on donations to identifiable and statistical victims', *Organizational Behavior and Human Decision Processes*, Vol. 102 pp 143–53

Morand, D. A. (2000), 'Language and power: an empirical analysis of linguistic strategies used in superior–subordinate communication', *Journal of Organizational Behavior*, Vol. 21 pp 235–48

Mutlu, B., Forlizzi, J. & Hodgins, J. (2006), 'A Storytelling Robot: Modeling and Evaluation of Human-like Gaze Behavior', IEEE-RAS International Conference, Genova, pp 518–23

Conley, J. M., O'Barr, W. M. & Lind, E. A. (1979), 'The Power of Language: Presentational Style in the Courtroom', *Duke Law Journal*, Vol. 27 No. 6 pp 1375–1400

## See also

Chapters 5 and 26 – **Fast and hard** looks at how the way you speak when you tell your stories affects things; as does the chapter **It's grim up north**

Chapter 12 – Stories make it easier for people to take on information. See **Overloaded**

Chapter 32 – The chapter **Telling stories** also looks at using stories in your presentations

## Further reading

If you want to get to grips with creating 'your organization's story, try John A. McLaughlin and Gretchen B. Jordan's 'Logic Models: A tool for telling your program's performance story' in *Evaluation and Program Planning*, Vol. 22 Issue 1 pp 65–72.

Sparkol is quite a nice piece of software for creating computer animations – you may have seen their work because the 'drawing hand effect' is quite popular now. Their blog is also pretty handy sometimes, and in particular you could spend time at: http://www.sparkol.com/blog/8-classic-storytelling-techniques-for-engaging-presentations

For almost any situation, you can rely on the TED website. Try this talk by J. J. Abrams, film director: http://www.ted.com/talks/j_j_abrams_mystery_box. Not only does he talk about storytelling, but you get to see him doing it.

# 17 THE VEXED PICTURE QUESTION

*How should we balance images and text?*

Most business presentations I've seen have used slides (usually from PowerPoint®, for better or for worse) and I know a few people who even go so far as to make the distinction between a presentation and a speech as to whether or not slides are used. They assume that one does not do an 'after-dinner presentation' with slides any more than one does a 'business speech' without them.

What that means for a presenter is that there's a bit of an issue about when to use images and when to use text – and in what combination – on their slides.

The term 'modality effect' is used in multimedia settings to suggest that people learn differently from the combination of pictures and spoken words than written words (text). This isn't automatically a problem – and can even be a good thing in many situations – but I've tended to look at the times when it's a problem for the sake of what I'm talking about here. This was exactly the area that interested a combination of researchers at Portuguese and German institutions, whose starting point was based upon various pieces of previous research:

- students learn better from pictures combined with spoken text (rather than written text)
- a modality effect only surfaces if the learning is complex or if information is presented at a speed that 'the system' controls rather than the student

- newcomers to a subject were particularly susceptible to the modality effect, whereas experts actually learned better with pictures with written text (this might well be related to the observation that if people know the subject well enough, they can ignore the picture)
- given the chance, a lot of people ignore images anyway, on the assumption that they don't hold much information
- simple pictures mitigate any problem cases by the modality effect – presumably because they don't clog up much of the working memory compared to a complicated picture
- people learn better from text and pictures rather than just text (probably because having both means that people can do some cross-referencing)
- listeners tend to grab the bigger picture (no pun intended) while readers tend to concentrate more on the details (for longer pieces of text).

So far, so good – there's nothing there that would surprise us and from a presenter's point of view it leads us towards the obvious conclusion that slides should contain relatively little text. Instead, we should use content-rich images and speak the commentary out loud, rather than have it appear on the screen.

There's quite a lot of discussion about the causes of the modality effect. It's possible to produce it by limiting how much time people have to take in information (such as by moving on through slides too quickly), which has been interpreted as meaning the effect is caused by a limit on how quickly people can move information into their 'working memory'. Others point to the idea that because working memory fades quickly if it's not reinforced, the modality effect is caused by the inevitable effort caused by splitting attention between verbal and visual information, leaving less mental capacity for doing other things, such as reinforcing your working memory.

The evidence for this second idea is supported by the fact that putting text and images physically close to each other reduces the modality effect, so that there's less effort needed to shift from text to images and back again, over and over. No matter how closely things are laid out, however, the effect never goes away if you're using written text. The only way around it, as a presenter, is to have verbal information instead of written stuff.

I like to think of this by analogy – and one that perhaps reflects my age but I'm sure you'll recognize this when I say that sometimes I go upstairs and forget what it was I went up for. Sometimes even going through a door to another room does it. Occasionally, even opening up another piece of software on my computer does it – I can't remember what I was going to use that software for... the physical interruption interrupts my memory, just like shifting attention from an image to text at the far side of the screen.

Schnotz et al moved our understanding along a bit when they carried out a number of experiments with students looking at information about plate tectonics, varying three things (giving a 2 by 2 by 2 matrix of results to analyse). They varied:

I have a personal confession to make here – I got particularly excited about the research in this paper because they used an example taken from a geography textbook... and both my undergraduate degree and PhD were from a department of geography. Yes, I know. I'm sad. But that isn't the only reason for looking at the results here.

- picture novelty – by showing the students the images before or after they were described
- auditory vs visual text – whether participants listened to text or read it
- picture-related vs content-related – in the latter, the words used talked about the same subject as the image in question (plate tectonics) whereas, for the picture-related content, the words talked much more about the picture, using it to explore the content.

Finding out how well people had learned under each of those different combinations of conditions is easy – just test people for how much they understood. Simple. And the results are pretty clear. When the words were about the picture, there was a noticeable modality effect but when the text was about plate tectonics directly there wasn't. What's more, when the picture was novel (that is, it hadn't been seen for as long) the effect was greater.

From a presenter's point of view, it means that if you're going to talk about the picture, it's better to let people look at that picture before you talk about it; and that you should talk about it rather than make people read about it.

Of course, as Schnotz et al are at pains to point out, this is one series of experiments about one topic and making generalized assumptions is dangerous. But if they're right, the advice for presenters is clear. If you expect a high modality effect, corresponding text should be spoken, not written – and you can make estimates of whether or not that's likely to be the case if the material is new; the pictures are complex; or there's a lot of linkage between the text and the image.

Of course, I wonder when a presenter would *not* be using new material. After all, if it's familiar to your audience, why are you presenting it? And if there's not much semantic connection between your words and the picture, what's the picture doing there in the first place? Prettiness has its place, I'm sure, but not here.

## So what are the big takeaways here?

- Create slides that have images and limit the number of words you use.
- If you do use text, try to integrate it reasonably with the picture and give your audience time to assimilate images before you work with it, if you can.
- Use simple-to-grasp pictures rather than detailed complicated ones. On a personal note, I find that it's possible to use complicated images if various complications are faded in to the picture a bit at a time, after the audience members have got their heads around what's on the screen so far – thus the complicated picture is incrementally built up from what you can think of as a number of simple pictures.

## Source

Schnotz, W., Mengelkamp, C., Baadte, C. & Hauck, G. (2014), 'Focus of attention and choice of text modality in multimedia learning', *European Journal of Psychology of Education* Vol. 29 Issue 3 pp 483–501

## See also

Chapters 6 and 9 – **It's not what you say, it's the way that you say it** reveals more about using figures and images in your presentations. So does **Diagram design**

Chapter 24 – Multimedia is also represented in **The best of PowerPoint®** – and sadly its worst, too

Chapter 37 – **Moving pictures** are perhaps the most blatant application of multimedia

## Further reading

To get a broader idea of how varied multimedia is, take five minutes to look behind the scenes at a TED conference. (It's not important what the conference is about or even that you know what TED is – just look at the range of media people are using!) http://blog.ted.com/2014/03/19/behind-the-scenes-gallery-day-3

# 18 FIT TO TALK?

*Does exercise and fitness help you when you're a presenter?*

Zoladz and Pilc are scientists working in Poland, and they've taken a good hard look at the effects of exercise on the human body. Some of their work was published in the *Journal of Physiology and Pharmacology* in 2010.

Zoladz and Pilc open their paper with a big bold statement, saying: 'It is well known that physical activity provides a number of various stimuli which are able to enhance both the metabolic and functional status of the human body.' They then go on to review a lot of the previous research – a lot of it carried out on rats – and start to move on to people-based research.

In particular they're interested in a specific protein that increases lots of functions, some related to learning and memory. It's called the 'brain-derived neurotrophic factor',

A big issue scientists have in this field is in moving from research on animals to humans. Setting aside the moral questions, there are things that scientists can do with animals that are harder to achieve when it comes to humans. Of necessity, research involving people tends to be more inferential and – quite often – not as advanced as what we know about animals.

So treat a lot of the claims you might read in the press with a pinch of salt. It's dangerously easy to get carried away and infer far more than science currently supports.

but fortunately for everyone the acronym BDNF will do. To cut a long story short, a lot of different pieces of research have a common trend, which is that bouts of exercise can increase levels of BDNF in the body. Each paper they look at has a slightly different way of making people exercise – such as sprinting until exhaustion (for around about three minutes, apparently) or 30 minutes of cycling at around two-thirds of the maximum capacity of their human guinea pigs. There are exceptions, of course, but generally speaking the 'storyline' remains the same: exercise makes you function better.

As presenters, it clearly pays to be fit.

Also in 2010, three researchers publishing in the journal *Neuroscience* were looking at the relationship between exercise and any benefits to learning and memory. Clearly both of these things are going to be handy to presenters and their audiences. The three researchers (Berchtold, Castello and Cotman) were particularly interested in how long the boost that exercise gives you can last. The good news is that is amounts to 'days'.

In mice at least!

What presenters need is an exercise routine that can be used as a short, sharp shock treatment for nerves and anxiety. Enter the concept of PMR, or Progressive Muscle Relaxation, or more recently a shortened version called, with no imagination at all, Abbreviated Progressive Muscle Relaxation, or APMR. Perhaps because it's free and relatively easy to self-administer there has been a huge amount of interest in APMR, including clinical trials on everything from stoma surgery patients to people suffering from anxiety neurosis, cancer, Alzheimer's and schizophrenia. Almost all have been at least partially successful.

Without wishing to imply that presenters are more like college students than clinical patients, one of the most relevant and useful examples of the research looked at highly stressed students at a US university. Some 546 students applied to be part of the research (which might say something about stress levels at the university), but only 136 were finally included: the rest were rejected because they weren't stressed enough, were using medications or were pregnant. Those who were left were randomly split into two groups.

The researchers used specially trained assistants to administer a 20-minute APMR session to approximately half the volunteers, using a standard script and aiming for similar pace, volume of voice and tone, etc. while the non-experiment group was asked to lie down, close their eyes and breathe freely. The idea was to replicate the APMR group's behaviour for everything *except* the APMR to deal with placebo effects: the experimenters even went so far as to tell the non-APMR group (the control group, just lying on the floor) that this was the 'treatment' to standardize as far as possible for any Hawthorne effect, too. (The Hawthorne effect is the tendency for things to change just because they're being looked at, in the way that blood pressure can sometimes increase simply by the anxiety caused by having it measured.)

The long and the short of the results is that while both groups tended to show a decrease in stress, etc., the group doing the APMR showed a statistically significant greater change. And it wasn't just in things like self-reported stress either: blood pressures dropped too. As the paper puts it: 'APMR intervention can have significant short-term effects by both reducing detrimental responses and enhancing restorative responses.'

As presenters, particularly novice presenters, anything that can help deal with nerves and performance anxiety can only be a good thing. The big question that all of this leads to, of course, is how to do it. What actually is an APMR?

The original idea comes from work in 1929 by a Chicago physician called Edmund Jacobson, but his version is inconveniently long for the modern world. To be honest, the details of how to do it can vary considerably: I've even created my own script, mixed with a little visualization, but the main points are that you should:

- find a safe, warm, comfortable place to work; it's hard to relax if you're anxious about being interrupted
- allow yourself 20 to 30 minutes
- lie down on your back; make sure your head is supported comfortably
- raise a leg, keeping it relatively straight and tip your foot back so that the muscles down your legs are tight; pay attention to that tension; hold things for about five seconds or so
- lower the leg to the floor and consciously relax it
- repeat for the other leg

- make a fist of your right hand; consciously pay attention to the tightness and tension in your forearm. Bend your arm and tighten your bicep: concentrate on that
- relax your bicep and your fist and consciously notice the difference
- repeat that for your other arm
- tighten your facial muscles by stretching up your eyebrows and pay attention to where feels tight, then relax and notice the difference
- do the same sort of thing to your eyes – both together: really screw them up tight
- clench your jaw and bite your teeth together and notice the tightness before you relax.

I usually find it handy to take a very short break, perhaps even standing up for a moment or two or looking out of the window (just to take my mind off things and hit a metaphorical 'reset' button) before starting again for one last step:

- repeat the process you've run through so far.

I also find it very helpful to finish off a session with a few minutes of mindfulness. I tend to think of mindfulness as being a kind of APMR for the brain.

One note of caution. If you do the exercises fully, resting on the floor, the chances are that you'll relax quite a bit – so much so that if you stand up in a hurry you risk what doctors call 'postural hypotension'. That's the fancy term for what most of us call 'head rush' or 'leaving our blood behind'.

If it happens to you, just wait a few moments until your heart sorts it all out or, better still, get up slowly, so that you don't get the effect.

## So what are the big takeaways here?

- **Exercise.** It's good for you anyway, so what have you got to lose?
- **Learn how to carry out an APMR and practise so that you can do it relatively quickly.**
- **Run through an APMR before your presentation.** Mix it up with a short period of mindfulness if you find that helpful.

## Sources

Zoladz, J. A. & Pilc, A. (2010), 'The effect of physical activity on the brain derived neurotrophic factor: from animal to human studies', *Journal of Physiology and Pharmacology*, Vol. 61 No. 5 pp 533–41

Berchtold, N. C., Castello, N. & Cotman, C. W. (2010), 'Exercise and time-dependent benefits to learning and memory', *Neuroscience*, Vol. 167 No. 3 pp 588–97

Dolbier, C. L. & Rush, T. E. (2012), 'Efficacy of Abbreviated Progressive Muscle Relaxation in a High-Stress College Sample', *International Journal of Stress Management*, Vol. 19 No. 1 pp 48–68

## See also

Chapter 36 – For another way of handling nerves, this time mentally, see **Minding what you say**

Chapter 39 – Sadly, being nervous can affect your sleep. Does it matter? See **Getting to bed**

## Further reading

An easy-to-read approach comes from *The Telegraph* newspaper: http://www.telegraph.co.uk/news/health/news/9090981/Regular-exercise-can-improve-memory-and-learning.html

It doesn't even have to be a long programme of exercise. There is some evidence that even one 'episode' of exercise helps improve your 'episodic memory'. (Episodic memory is the memory of events.) See: http://www.sciencedirect.com/science/article/pii/S0001691814001577

# 19 DOCTORS KNOW BEST

*What can we learn from how doctors are trained?*

Let's be honest, I'm biased here. I've spent a lot of my working life among medical doctors (although I am not a medical doctor myself), working with them on joint research projects and so on, as well as training them in how to make presentations (for a while I was even the trainer for a company called Public Speaking for Doctors, which managed to misspell my name on its marketing material!). Some of my closest friends are medics and even my daughter is a doctor. Frankly, my impression of them is mixed. What I can't argue with, however, is that they're very keen on evidence (like all of us, of course, it helps if that evidence matches what they wanted it to say…). That means that quite a bit of research has been done into how people learn in an evidence-based way and one of the leaders in this field is Richard Mayer from the Department of Psychology at the University of California.

Over the years, he's done a lot of work in this field – enough, in fact, to mean that when I settled down to read all his work in my favourite cafe, it turned out to be very expensive few days. (I can drink a lot of chai latte in a week.)

In a piece of summary work (I wish I'd found this first!) from 2010, Mayer wraps up the different kinds of things your presentation might need to cover as at least one of five things:

- facts – X is smaller than Y
- concepts – X causes Y when Z applies
- procedures – what to do when X causes Y
- strategies – long-term approaches to the relationship between X and Y
- beliefs – I understand what to do about X and Y and I'm good at dealing with it.

I've not done much by way of making suggestions about exercises in this book but here's one – take a few minutes to go through your last presentation and see which bits of it fit into each of these five categories. Some bits, of course, will blur the lines, but I find that happens less often than you might expect. However, in order to apply what you learn in a presentation you usually need all five. That, in turn, means that it's possible to test two types of outcomes from a presentation – retention tests measure how much your audience has learned and remembered of what you've said when you make your presentation; and transfer tests, test how well your audience can apply what you've said in different situations.

I've captured the implications of the different results in the table.

| | Low retention scores | High retention scores |
|---|---|---|
| Low transfer scores | People can neither recall nor apply what you've said. You know you've done a really bad presentation if this is what you get. You've wasted everyone's time (including your own!). | Rote learning. If people can remember what you've said but not apply it, they've probably not understood it at a useful level. |
| High transfer scores | To be honest, I don't think this is possible – or at least if it is, it's more because of your audience's innate intelligence than anything you've done. You've got lucky. | This is what you're aiming for. People remember a lot, and can apply it. |

Mayer summarizes all the various complexities of his work in a single metric called the 'Effect Size' (ES) to look at how strong an effect various phenomena have: an effect size of more than 0.5 is regarded as a good result and I've included Mayer's ES scores in brackets, below. The first three are for reducing how much unnecessary mental effort people have to do when they're in presentations (or in the case of this research, being instructed).

First, people learn better when **extraneous information is omitted:** that sounds obvious since why would you simply add random detail to anything, anyway? But when you start applying it to presentations, it means that you consider using schematic, representational figures rather than photographs. The more simple schematics make it easier for people to see what's important, to see the wood for the trees (*ES 0.97*).

My personal experience is that the majority of presentations concentrate on just giving people information far, far too much. You might get higher retention scores that way but you're sacrificing your transfer scores.

The alternative extreme, of giving people too much time to assimilate and practise what they're learning, risks not covering enough ground in your presentation...

Second, people learn better when the session highlights the essential material by using **headings or words that signpost the structure** of what you're saying: the example here might be the way I used the word 'second' at the start of this sentence, and how I'm going to start the next sentence with the obvious one (*ES 0.52*).

...well let's just say it's not a common enough problem for me to lose sleep over it.

Third, people learn better when **labels and what they're labelling are contiguous.** (This is covered in a bit more detail in the chapter 'Diagram design' but for now, imagine how much harder a map is to read if the city names aren't right next to the dots that represent them (*ES 1.19*).)

If the first three principles are about reducing *unnecessary* mental effort, Mayer's next three principles all concern reducing the *necessary* mental effort.

The first of these is called 'pre-training'. This is the idea that people find it **easier to learn if they're already familiar with key concepts.** For example, it's easier to understand how a bike's gearing system works if you're already familiar with terms such as 'gear' and 'cog' (*ES 0.98*). As a presenter you might consider doing things like using a handout before your presentation starts, with certain key definitions included on it, or making sure that you don't use unfamiliar jargon.

The next principle is that things **should be broken down into chunks which are small** enough for people to get their heads around in one go. (You might also think about letting your audience control how fast you go on to the next chunk, too.) An analogy that helps me with this one is that I can't wrap my head around how to write a computer program to work out the shortest route by bus from my house to a friend's, but I'm perfectly happy writing something to 1) get the data, 2) then to sort that data and 3) to check the data for errors, before 4)… I'm sure you get the idea (*ES 0.85*).

The third principle in this group is that **words should be spoken, not written**. This is simply because people often have more spare brain capacity in what is called their 'auditory-verbal channel' and can generally process speech better than a handout, for example (*ES 1.02*).

As a presenter, it's pretty easy to see how to use these ideas – the trick lies in having the mental self-discipline to go through the content of your presentation and break it into appropriate sized chunks, etc. It's very easy to say things rather than have your audience read things – you just have to remember to do it.

The third set of three principles are all to do with helping people make sense of what they've heard and seen – technically referred to as 'principles for fostering generative processing'.

The first of these is covered elsewhere and it's to **present words and pictures rather than words alone** (*ES 1.39*).

The second principle is the 'personalization principle' and it's exactly what you would expect – **when you talk, do so in a relatively personal, informal way**. Talking about 'the heart' is less effective than talking about 'your heart'. I'm not sure it's grammatically, absolutely, perfectly correct all the time, but no one ever died from an overdose of colloquialism (*ES 1.11*).

Personally, I think it's a shame to end on a whimper, but the last principle, of **using a real person rather than a machine's voice**, doesn't often apply to the types of presentations I've sat through.

None of these principles are difficult in and of themselves – you just have to make a point of looking at your presentation with them in mind. An approach I recommend is to take a moment to think about which of the principles relate to designing and structuring your presentation and which apply to delivering your presentation, then jot them down on index cards (or something similar) and have the relevant 'design' cards (but only the relevant cards, in accordance with the principles themselves) in front of you as you design your presentation. Then when you're done, tidy them away and give yourself a break before you go on. When you're ready, put the principles relating to delivery up in front of you and go through each and every slide or spoken paragraph in your presentation one at a time and challenge it to live up to each principle. Personally, I find I need to do this bit a couple of times, as it's simply too big to do it all at once.

So far I've presented a summary of Mayer's work but it might be helpful to wrap up with an example. In 2011, Mayer worked with a veritable army of co-authors to look at the effect of applying multimedia design principles to some third-year medical students' lectures at a private university. Starting with cohorts who had pretty similar levels of knowledge about shock, two groups were given traditional lectures, while two received modified lectures.

Both groups improved (which is reassuring for the people paying for the education of these students) and did so in both tests for retention and transfer. However, the group that received the modified lectures, based on the principles I've outlined here, improved more, particularly for the retention test. In other words, the students learned more when the style of lecture was changed to follow Mayer's principles. In fairness, I should point out that the results for the two groups didn't differ for the transfer tests, suggesting that although they learned more, students didn't get any better at knowing what to do with the extra information – but that's a problem for another chapter.

## So what are the big takeaways here?

- Familiarize yourself with the nine (three groups of three) principles so that you're not trying to learn them and apply them at the same time.
- Have the relevant principles in front of you as you firstly design and then subsequently edit your presentation.
- Go over your presentation repeatedly, looking at each individual bit of it through the lens of each of the principles, looking for tweaks you can make to get closer to the ideal.

## Sources

Mayer. R. E. (2010), 'Applying the science of learning to medical education', *Medical Education*, Vol. 44 No. 6 pp 543–9

Issa, N., Schuller, M., Santacaterina, S., Shapiro, M., Wang, E, Mayer, R. E. & DaRosa, D. A. (2001), 'Applying multimedia design principles enhances learning in medical education', *Medical Education*, Vol. 45 No. 8 pp 818–26

## See also

Chapters 2 and 12 – Key concepts that this chapter builds on are explored in **You know that feeling when your head is full...** and **Overloaded**

Chapter 9 – Have a look at how to design your figures to make them easier for your audience: **Diagram design**

## Further reading

In a brilliantly titled talk, 'Talk Nerdy to Me' you can get a few ideas about how to present scientific ideas to non-scientific audiences: http://www.ted.com/talks/melissa_marshall_talk_nerdy_to_me

Being informal is fine: but that's different from bad English. This article from Suzan St Maur lists some of the mistakes speakers often make when they let their formal guard down: http://howtowritebetter.net/50-shades-of-bad-english-writing. The rest of the blog is worth checking out, too.

To see how badly things can go wrong when scientists don't explain things properly, just look at how out of balance the beliefs of Americans and American scientists have got – there's an easily readable summary here: www.pewinternet.org/2015/01/29/public-and-scientists-views-on-science-and-society

# 20 POWER OF PERSUASION

*How can you boost your influence from the front of the room?*

The man with the answers in the area of influence and persuasion is Professor Robert Cialdini. He's regarded as more or less the definitive authority in this area by, well, just about everyone. I urge you to read his seminal book, *Influence: Science and Practice*: it's an exceptionally engaging read that will change the way you look at adverts and marketing in general and, rather depressingly, make you realize that you have a lot less control over your own life than you might have supposed.

Cialdini was born in 1945 and is the Regents' Professor Emeritus of Psychology and Marketing at Arizona State University. Google (or other search engines) will turn up a plethora of articles by and about him – as well as many videos, some of which are an even quicker introduction to his work than the book. Cialdini reveals that there are six big principles that can be used to influence how people behave. Some of them have more obvious and immediate application to presenters and some of them are more easily applied as subtle, long-term tools.

Before he even gets into the details of his principle however, Cialdini makes some observations that are potentially very useful for presenters. Carefully researched, well-balanced and comprehensively informed decisions are time-consuming and probably expensive in other ways too. There's a lot of evidence that people use what are called 'judgement heuristics' to help them make decisions: the result is that we take mental short-cuts. At their worst, these can be things like assumptions and prejudices, but they're more subtle than that in most cases.

A typical example is taking price as a guide to value. If we have no other information to go on we assume that the more expensive an item is, the higher quality it is. As a professional speaker I can certainly testify to many anecdotes from my peers who have seen an increase in the number of bookings they have received after they have put their prices up.

Another example is taking the word of an expert. Simply putting the letters 'Dr' or 'Prof.' in front of my name can make it more likely that my opinion is taken seriously, all other things being equal. (Obviously this doesn't apply to circumstances that allow personal information to be applied as well. Calling myself Dr has absolutely no effect on whether my friends or family agree with me, for example!)

Ask yourself which of the following you assume to contain more reliable information:

- something I knocked up this morning
- research that was three years in the making, with another 18 months of writing up.

If it's the former I'd be surprised. And disappointed.

As a culture, we're also predicated to think that there's a logic to the world around us. In some entertaining research Cialdini reports that people are more likely to be able to cut into a queue, for example to use a photocopier, when the queue-jumper gives a reason. Importantly, it barely matters what the reason is: it can be as spurious as '...because I need to make some copies'.

Indeed – one wonders what else one would be doing at a photocopier.

Perhaps what this implies is that because the world is so big and complicated we can't process it all the time without going crazy, so we assume that any reason must be a good reason. After all, we wouldn't do things without a reason, so why would anyone else?

Once Cialdini gets into the flow of his six principles, there's a lot that a presenter can use, so I'll split it over a few chapters.

The very first of his principles is 'reciprocity'. Briefly stated (and horribly oversimplified), this is the idea that people pay back in kind if you do something for them – often disproportionately to the original deed. The research for this can be fun, such as sending Christmas cards to strangers and seeing if they send a card back, just because you sent one to them.

There's a more serious side, though, with some research suggesting that reciprocity is the single 'glue' that holds civilizations together. Pretty scary stuff in some ways and Cialdini gives example after example of this rule at work: without thinking about it, we're being manipulated to behave in certain ways and to like certain people...

If you're not convinced, think on a more personal level; think about who gets invited to children's parties – the children who invited your child to their party. And you don't think that the waiter gives you sweets or mints when they give you the bill just because they like you, do you? No, it's because you're about to decide how much to tip them. If they've given you something, the average tip will be higher.

On a personal level I can attest to giving people time off in the week, only for them to work more than the extra hours back over the next week. As a boss, it was a convenient way of being nice...

The limits seem to be that the initial thing you give them should not be ridiculous though – and must not be perceived as an attempt to 'buy favour': it has to feel genuine to the recipient. And, of course, it's (as Cialdini himself puts it) 'unnecessary and undesirable in certain long-term relationships such as families or established friendships'. Unless you're in the habit of making presentations to your partner, children or parents, that seems to be good news for the presenter.

A friend of mine and a speaker in the same sort of area as me is Paul McGee. Google him as 'the SUMO guy' and you'll find him easily enough. Often, Paul gives away postcard-sized handouts for people to take away at the end of his presentations.

The postcards are a great idea because they do a lot of things simultaneously:

- provide audiences with an aide-mémoire of what Paul has said, to use later
- work as a possible bit of marketing as they get passed around or noticed on desks
- dispose the audience to think well of Paul – after all, he's given them something.

Now don't get me wrong. I'm not suggesting Paul is sufficiently Machiavellian to be thinking about the third of these (if I know Paul, he's more interested in the first than the second even!) but the effect is the same as if he were.

And me? I offer people two months' unlimited support by email after the presentation, in case anyone needs a bit of support...

## So what are the big takeaways here?

- **Using the idea that people equate cost and quality, you can make the obvious adjustments to your presentations.** Don't sell yourself short by starting your presentation with sentiments such as 'I'm not sure why I'm here...' or 'I'm not an expert in this area...'. We probably do it to lower expectations so that if our presentation is not that good we aren't so gutted about it – but unfortunately doing this makes it a little more likely the audience won't be impressed by our content.
- **Give your audience the weight of the evidence** – don't bore them to death with all the details of your backup data but make sure the audience knows that there *is* backup data. A simple line that you interviewed 94 per cent of all the relevant people, for example, lends gravitas: and so does letting your audience know that your research took three years and not just one morning.
- **Provide your reasoning.** People like to be given reasons. Sometimes all you have to do is use the word 'because'. The justification that comes after it isn't as important as the fact that there is a justification.

- **Think about what you can give your audience, preferably before your presentation starts.** If, like Paul McGee, you decide to go for postcards, then great. If not, use a bit of imagination. The key thought to hold on to is that it should not look like you're trying to ingratiate yourself, but at the same time it shouldn't be something the audience would automatically expect (so just passing out your handouts won't do, no matter how well crafted, written and ring-bound they may be).

## Source

Cialdini, Robert B., *Influence: Science and Practice* (Pearson Education Ltd., Harlow, 2003)

## See also

Chapter 3 – Influence is predicated on trust, and simplicity of delivery helps trust grow. See **Clarity is king**

Chapters 21 and 22 – Cialdini's book is a rich source for presenters – there are two other chapters to look at: **Being more persuasive** and **And more persuasive still**

## Further reading

Paul McGee's website has a host of helpful blog posts and downloads at: www.thesumoguy.com

Pat Fripp is one of the high flyers of the professional speaking world and her blog has plenty of useful stuff. You can start here, with a brief reference to reciprocity: http://www.fripp.com/blog/why-do-people-say-yes-the-6-weapons-of-influence

# BEING MORE PERSUASIVE

*What other tricks can we learn from the marketeers?*

Professor Robert Cialdini's second principle is called 'commitment and consistency'. (So, in the spirit of consistency, make sure you've read Chapter 20 before you get going here.) In short, people don't like being inconsistent. That's no surprise, but what does surprise people is that we resolve internal conflict in two ways. If we find ourselves acting counter to what we believe, we change what we're doing. Great. Less reassuringly, however, there's a lot of evidence that at least some of the time we change what we believe so that it fits what we're currently doing.

I've known people who've convinced themselves of the most absurd things, simply because they couldn't face the alternative. One of my friends insists that smoking is good for her: she's not stupid and she's not unaware of the fact that it's bad for everyone else, but it's good for her. Why? Because she smokes – and rather than stop smoking she's closed her mind to evidence that overwhelms anyone who's able to listen to it.

I might speculate that a lot of religious debate and political argument suffers from the same problem. People vote for party

I heard a news report this morning that various organizations were claiming a national referendum in Scotland (about whether to secede from the rest of the United Kingdom) had not actually taken place. I have friends who voted: it is inconceivable that the vote did not occur and yet there are apparently organizations who are so mired in their beliefs, because of their actions, that they convince themselves that the BBC perpetrated a fraud by pretending the referendum took place – so as to sow sedition in the areas controlled by these organizations.

X for some reason or another and thereby become unable to 'hear' evidence that suggests they should vote for party Y.

This principle is why people are more likely to turn up to do something if they've signed up for it, rather than having been involved passively (by not unchecking a tickbox, for example).

I was on the receiving end of it this morning, from a chugger (a street collector working for a charity, a so-called 'charity mugger'). Here's how the conversation went:

**Chugger:** Hi – can I ask you a couple of questions?

**Me:** (vague agreeing sound)

**Chugger:** I work for XXX and I'd be interested to know if you think it's right that so many children die of malnutrition and starvation every day..?

**Me:** No, of course not.

**Chugger:** No, of course... and presumably you think we should be doing something to save their lives?

**Me:** Yes

**Chugger:** And would the people best placed to do that be the people who are better off?

**Me:** Yeah, sure. Obviously.

**Chugger:** Well as we're standing on YYY Street, I think we count as better off, don't you?

**Me:** I guess...

**Chugger:** So would you like to donate £ZZZ per month to our work so we can combat the malnutrition?

**Me:** ...

Clearly the alarm bells should have started ringing pretty early in that conversation, because with only a little forethought it's pretty obvious where it's going. In my defence, I was on the way to the library early on a Saturday morning to work on this book and my brain was still in bed. Other, more subtle examples abound. Cialdini describes it as being as if the need to be consistent is more important than thinking for yourself: it's a tool that means you can avoid the hard work of figuring out what you actually believe, simply by looking at what you're currently doing and passively assuming that you must have thought it through at some point in the past so you don't need to work it all out again.

It can, of course, have positive uses. On a personal note, one of the ways I fitted in writing this book around my other work was by committing time in my diary to doing the (often tedious) research I needed to do. Once it was in my diary it became my default action to do what the electronic genie was nagging me to do. (As an aside, my wife can also add things to my diary using her smartphone – it turns out it's a great way for her to set my default behaviour too!) As a presenter, the rhetorical approaches are pretty obvious: people are more likely to do things if they agree to do them in public and – importantly – if it's couched in terms that make things consistent with what they've already said and/or agreed to.

A simple example might be helpful. I was recently asked to make a presentation to a team who were in siege mode; they felt picked on and underappreciated so that they resented any attempts to help them, assuming it wouldn't work or was a trick. Before I began to explore any of the tools I had that might help, I got the audience to publicly (by raising their hands) agree that they'd try a tool if they felt that it *might* help. And at the end of showing people six tools I got them to vote on the one that was most immediately applicable, making it more likely that they'll try it out.

Even the British Government has got in on using the principle. The Behavioural Insights Team (often called the 'Nudge Unit' because it looks for ways to nudge us into more acceptable behaviour) was established in 2010. Things they've been involved with include a smoking cessation pilot from 2011, which requires people to sign a contract about quitting smoking, and so on. Perhaps more significantly, millions of pounds per year can be saved by rolling out such apparently simple things as getting people to sign their tax information at the beginning of a form rather than at the end. Once someone has signed to say that they're going to be honest it's harder to lie than if they had filled in the form first and then signed to say they haven't lied.

At its most simple, this principle shows that once we have given our word, we keep it. (But the key is that we actively give it, not just have it assumed for us.) How many times have you found yourself going to some social event that sounded like a good idea when you accepted the invitation but you wished you could skip as the time draws near: 'I've got to go. I promised Sue that I would.'

From a presenter's point of view, not only can you use this as part of your rhetoric, you can also use it to control the room. For example, if you get people to agree to the rule of 'no mobile phones' rules up front, before it's needed, you are in a much stronger position than if you try to control events as and when they happen. People are less likely to be difficult if they've given a public affirmation that they won't be.

Let's move on to Cialdini's next principle – social proof.

Put simply, this is the idea that we all like to do what everyone else is doing. With my tongue in my cheek I'd like to ask you what you do when someone comes into the office with a charity sponsorship form. They're about to bungee off the nearest high bridge or something and they give you the form – and a pen (remember the principle of reciprocity?) and wait for you to sign up. What's the first thing you do?

Typically, it would be to check the amounts sponsored by the other people on the form already. You want to see how much you're 'supposed' to be sponsoring – what's normal?

Essentially, social proof stems from the idea that in the grand scheme of things (as my mother used to say) if you don't know what to do, the best thing to do is what everyone else is doing. You might not change the world that way, but you'll at least not make a fool of yourself. Cialdini gives some astonishing examples of the power of fitting in this way – everything from judging the size of a tip to curing phobias to waiting for the end of the world to committing suicide.

No one is suggesting that your presentations are so bad that they make your audience want to defect or kill themselves, but the tool can be applied by the presenter very handily. Essentially, all you have to do is to decide what you want your audience to do and then make it appear normal to them to do it.

Why else do you think sitcoms have (bad!) dubbed laughter? We all know that it's false and dubbed in after the recording, but the research says the best way to make people laugh is to get them to join in with other people who are already laughing. Sad, I know.

Another book on the topic, *The Lucifer Effect* by Philip Zimbardo, tells the story of a psychology experiment where a fake prison was created: the experiment had to be aborted early as the guards involved became so wrapped up in their roles that things became dangerous. One could make a strong case to suggest that there was a lot of 'social proof' at work here both in how the guards became ever-more repressive and how the prisoners (volunteers all, remember!) become cowed. I discuss this further in the chapter, The Lucifer Effect.

Perhaps even sadder is the history of putting 'ringers' in theatres. At one stage, you could find adverts for 'claqueurs' who would applaud according to a fee.

There's a lesson there for presenters, depending on your moral position!

In terms of how to use this in what you say, consider normalizing the behaviour you want to encourage in your audience. For example, if you want to finish your presentation with a question-and-answer session, you might want to consider avoiding the terrifying moment of tumbleweed, when no one asks anything, simply by having a couple of confederates in the audience primed to ask a question if no one else does to get things off the ground.

You could also think about keying someone up to start applause at the end of your presentation, if it's that kind of presentation. I stop short of suggesting you pay friends to stand up cheering 'encore!' but once the applause is started it allows other people to join in.

One final (if obvious) word. Social proof will backfire if people suspect it is faked. Quite right, too.

## So what are the big takeaways here?

- **Get your audience to agree to the rules up front.** An example I often use is to do with confidentiality. Another is when we're going to take breaks and when we can handle questions.
- **Remember that the members of your audience are there because they want to be.** That means they're already committed to the presentation being a success. They don't want it to be a waste of their time (although many of them might expect it will be, but that's a different issue). Use that. First, you can use it to help calm your nerves, just by knowing it, but, second, also by getting your audience to agree that they're going to be given (say) six tools for improving time management and before you start explaining them you'd 'like them to agree to use just even one of them during the next week. Fair?'. Putting your hand up to encourage them to do the same adds another layer of effect as they, in effect, sign their names by raising their hands.
- **Depending on the kind of presentation you're giving, a good case study (or survey) can provide a lot of powerful social proof.** But make absolutely sure that the people in your audience will identify with the people involved in the case study: there's little point in providing a case study about female 13-year-old violin virtuosos to male 34-year-old computer programmers who would rather die than perform in front of an audience...

## Source

Cialdini, Robert B., *Influence: Science and Practice* (Pearson Education Ltd., Harlow, 2003)

## See also

Chapters 20 and 22 –There are two other chapters on Cialdini: **Power of persuasion** and **And more persuasive still**

Chapter 23 – There's a whole chapter dedicated to **The Lucifer Effect**

## Further reading

You can get your own copy of *The Lucifer Effect* (2008) by Philip Zimbardo, published by Rider.

The UK Government has done some good work on how to use these effects to get people to be more honest when they fill in tax returns, for example, see: https://www.gov.uk/government/uploads/system/uploads/attachment_data/file/60539/BIT_FraudErrorDebt_accessible.pdf

# 22 AND MORE PERSUASIVE STILL

*Is it more important that audiences like the presenter or that they respect him or her?*

Cialdini moves on: liking is next. Obviously, people are more likely to be positively inclined to people they know and like – in no small part because their friends will tend to be like them.

There are a number of components to this 'liking' that a presenter should be aware of:

- physical attractiveness
- similarity
- compliments
- contact and cooperation.

Let's take them in turn.

**Physical attractiveness** is pretty obvious, right? Well, yes, but it turns out that it's even more effective in getting cooperation from people than might be expected. Good-looking political candidates are more electable; good looks in job candidates are often more important than their qualifications; good-looking employees statistically earn more; good-looking defendants in court cases tend to get lighter sentences; the list goes on.

No one is suggesting you get plastic surgery before you become a presenter, but the evidence suggests that making the best of yourself is more important than we might think (a lot more important). Perhaps helpfully, Cialdini reports that there's an element of association that's important too – just being seen with good-looking people will help. If you can't afford plastic surgery, consider hiring an attractive assistant.

The problem with looks is that most people are pretty close to average looking, more or less by definition but that's fine because Cialdini reports that we have a tendency to like people who we regard as similar to us. That's handy, because similarity is something a presenter can modify more easily than their looks (or at least how similarity is *perceived* by the audience can be modified).

Now to **similarity**. I used to work a lot as a lighting designer for dance companies, going into theatres before the dancers arrived and asking the hard-bitten, cynical and underpaid technical staff of the theatre to put the lights where I wanted them for my design. Imagine me walking into the theatre wearing a suit, tie and freshly polished shoes, asking for the two thousand watt fresnel lantern to be re-rigged on front of house lighting bar number two.

Now imagine me wearing cut-off jeans, trainers and an old rock band t-shirt, and saying: 'Sling the knackered two-k frezzi on LX2, guys.'

You can guess which gets more response, I'm sure...

**Compliments,** it turns out, work pretty well, even if the receiver knows that the person giving the compliments has something to gain. What's even harder to swallow is that research suggests the compliment doesn't even have to be accurate to work. (Obviously, I do mean it when I say I like my wife's new glasses or she has a great new hairstyle.) Personally, I'd be careful with overdoing it, but it should be pretty clear how a good presenter like you can use this tool. And you are a good presenter, no question.

Finally comes **contact and cooperation** – which basically means we tend to like things that are familiar to us. Why? Well possibly because, at the evolutionary level, if it's familiar to us it means it hasn't eaten us. If you can make yourself seem familiar to your audience, you're onto a winner: even something as familiar as an easy-to-pronounce-name can be useful. (Smith is easier than Smyth-Hempleton, for example.) Don't start your presentations with something too wacky: if you're going to do things that make people uncomfortable, don't do it at the start of your presentation. (You'd be amazed at how many professionals slip up here, thinking they need to make a big impact and start with a bang!)

There are two more of Cialdini's principles to consider, **authority** and **scarcity**. In short, the former means we conform to authority or symbols of authority, and the latter means we want things simply because we can't have them. Simple, eh?

How powerful are these two effects? Authority can (and has) been used in experiments to get people to administer electric shocks powerful enough to make the victims scream, writhe and beg to be released. (It was faked, don't worry, but the person doing the electrocuting didn't know that.)

Even the association of authority can be a powerful tool. Adding 'Dr', 'Professor' and/or other titles in front of your name are all you need to subtly shift people's responses (there are always exceptions, don't forget). The effect is so persuasive that research finds that the same man can be estimated to be about six centimetres taller when he's referred to as 'Professor'. Oh, and since 1900 the winning candidate in the US presidential election has been the taller of the two men nearly 90 per cent of the time: random chance would obviously predict a 50:50 pattern. Uniforms and other physical symbols of authority work pretty well, too, but – importantly – experiments also show that while we're all a sucker for a uniform, we all like to *think* we're immune.

And you know it's true because I'm telling you. And I'm a doctor. And I'm tall. And I'm wearing a suit. And I start my presentations by quoting Einstein. You might laugh, but all of them will increase your perceived authority in your audience's eyes.

## So what are the big takeaways here?

- **Consider making yourself accessible to your audience before the presentation.** Perhaps greet them at the door, find out a few names you can reference during your presentation e.g. 'as Dave was telling me before I came on stage…'
- **Dress like your audience.** If they're in business attire, then dress that way and associate yourself with something your audience members are familiar with. For example, your opening slide could contain your name and a version of the logo of the company you're presenting to.
- **Associate yourself with symbols and people that the audience recognizes as authorities.** For example, I regularly give guest lectures at Imperial College, a very prestigious university in London where I train research scientists in how to make presentations: it's no coincidence that one of my very early slides has a large facial picture of Albert Einstein. Nor is it a coincidence that when that slide is on, I stand next to the screen.

## Source

Cialdini, Robert B., *Influence: Science and Practice* (Pearson Education Ltd., Harlow, 2003)

## See also

Chapter 5 – The speed you speak at and even whether you swear or not can have an impact on how influential you are. Have a look at **Fast and hard**

Chapters 20-21 – This is the third chapter on Cialdini – see **Power of persuasion** and **Being more persuasive**

## Further reading

If you really want to see how effective the whole concept of 'authority' can be, do a web search for the famous Milgram experiment and ask yourself (honestly) what you would do if you were in those circumstances.

# 23 THE LUCIFER EFFECT

*Does your presentation's social context matter?*

*The Lucifer Effect* is the name of a book by Philip Zimbardo, which is as fascinating a read as it is depressing. The subtitle explains why it gets me down: 'How good people turn evil'.

Back in 1971 Professor Zimbardo ran the now infamous Stanford Prison Experiment (*The Lucifer Effect* was the first time that all the work associated with that experiment had been published.) You may be familiar with the bare bones of the experiment, as it has passed into something of Internet legend and almost everyone has heard some variation of the real story. Entering the words 'Stanford Prison Experiment' into Google produces over a third of a million hits – the very first one of which is the official website of the experiment that contains a brief suggestion of what the researchers were interested in, such things as: 'what happens when you put good people in an evil place?'

> This is a chapter that very nearly didn't make it into this book – not so much because of the moral issues of the research but because the research is much more extreme than anything you, as a presenter, will encounter (I sincerely hope so in any case!). That said, the principles of what the research shows can be transferable, so I hope you agree it's worth the risk of including it.

The site then goes on to give the stark facts. They had planned a two week 'investigation into the psychology of prison life' but in less than half that planned time, that is, only six days, the experiment had to be abandoned. Pretend guards in a pretend prison became sadistic, while pretend prisoners in a pretend prison became depressed; some of them became remarkably stressed and anxious.

Some of the most striking things to come from the research are that after only 36 hours in a pretend prison, one of the volunteer internees 'lost it' – he became emotionally ill. Only 36 hours; – wow! He was so ill that he was 'released'.

By day four, there were rumours of an attempted rescue by the released prisoner and his friends, which was perhaps not surprising. What certainly was surprising is that the reaction of the experimenters wasn't to simply observe (as they should have if they were doing well-structured research) but instead to get so protective of their 'prison' that they spent all day preparing for the 'revolution'. (It never came, by the way.)

By the way, none of this happened because the volunteers were particularly vulnerable. On the contrary, only 24 students of the 70 who replied to an advert were accepted, because of filtering out of anyone with possible psychological problems, or any history of drugs and so on.

Later in the experiment, a priest and a lawyer were both invited in. Both knew it was a mock-up, but both were so caught up in the reality that they slipped into their roles completely. So did the parents of the prisoners on visiting day, becoming complicit with the guards.

Towards the end of the experiment, a mock parole board ran in which the prisoners behaved like real prisoners, without hope and without the ability to think outside of the box (a rather literal one, on this occasion).

The point isn't so much the extremes of behaviour here (although there were certainly plenty of those) but rather the fact that the behaviours were so easily generated – simply by having a prison 'set' and some undergraduates acting as prisoners and guards.

For presenters, this offers us a lot of useful information about how we can expect audiences to behave. I'm often asked in my role as a presentation skills trainer how my clients can 'control' their audiences: essentially, people are frightened of not being able to cope with things like challenging questions or people being hostile in more passive ways. The answer, based upon this experiment, would seem to be pretty clear.

You should set things up in advance of the presentation to 'steer' your audience towards the behaviour you need. For example, I make a point of suggesting to my audience, as they come in, that they fill up from the front instead of skulking at the back as they prefer to try to do. Inevitably, they have to come forward and in the process of doing that, they effectively cede to me the authority role, rather like pretend prisoners ceding control to pretend guards.

Ask any teacher and they'll tell you the same. Once their pupils get to the challenging teenage years you can't actually control them. You act as though you're in charge and (usually) the pupils therefore behave as though you're in charge. As a presenter you could do the same with the expectation that mobile phones are off. Or perhaps you could even simply give out pens so that people can take notes, giving the clear expectation that they should, and therefore will.

Personally, I find it useful to have a 'splash screen' on before the audience arrives, so that they know what they're getting as they walk in (this displays the title of the presentation, and perhaps what time I expect to finish, or even a message such as 'Please turn off your mobile phones'). Whatever you do, it's simply a case of setting the physical scene right from the start, and backing it up by acting in the expectation of cooperation. Obviously that means you have to set up before the audience arrives, but you'd do that anyway, of course, simply out of courtesy for their time (it wastes their time for you to be fumbling with your remote control's batteries, trust me on this). It also undermines your credibility if the audience see you're working (if you don't believe me, watch *The Wizard of Oz*, when Dorothy exposes the wizard).

Perhaps an even more horrifying piece of research is the infamous Milgram experiment. Since it was published, some subsequent analysis has rather mitigated the full-blown effects of this particular combination of science and B-movie horror show, but the rather brutal main thrust of the work stands. So what was so horror-movie-esque (is that a real word?) about this particular piece of work? Try not to judge too harshly: 1963 was a different world…

Milgram arranged for 'teachers' to train 'learners' who were in a different room. There was also an authority figure in the room with the 'teacher': the 'learners' were in on it. With me so far? Each time the learner got a question wrong, the teacher was to give them an electric shock and every wrong answer also increased the voltage of the shock by 15 volts. In reality there were no shocks being administered and the sound-effects of receiving shocks were pre-recorded. The important point here, however, is that the teachers believed they were giving real shocks.

You've possibly heard the results of this rather byzantine piece of experimentation. The faked responses from the learner went up in stages, including things like banging on the wall, complaining about the problems with his heart condition and ultimately (and unbelievably, perhaps) suddenly not responding at all! If the teacher tried to back out, the researcher/authority figure in the room prompted them to continue. The really scary thing here is that when prompted by the authority figure, about two-thirds of people were prepared to administer a shock of 450 volts – that's the sort of level that can cause very severe problems (including a faked death from aggravating a heart condition in this experiment).

From a presenter's point of view, this is (horrific perhaps but nevertheless…) good news. It implies that people are rather taken with authority figures. (There's lots of other research into this that is less gruesome but correspondingly more realistic, to do with things like how many people do as they're told if the person giving instructions is wearing a uniform of some kind, for example.) Simply by being at the front, you're an authority figure. By sounding and acting credibly, you're an authority figure. By citing a 'high power' source for your evidence, you're an authority figure (but it's ethically important that it's real, of course – you might lose credibility if you cite Abraham Lincoln as one of your greatest fans, for example).

Don't forget, according to Cialdini (see the other chapters) you can even borrow authority, simply by wearing something representative of authority (such as a doctor wearing a white coat). From a presenter's point of view, this is all good news because it means you can establish your credibility with relatively little effort, simply by acting as though you've already got the authority.

On a personal basis, for example, while everything in my public speaking is carefully researched, no one has *ever* asked me for my sources (which I have as a handout, just in case) after I have briefly waved the handout at the start of my presentation saying something to the effect of '… and if you want the boring backup data, the references are all here – just ask me for them at the end'.

In an ideal world, of course, you'd get someone else to establish your authority. Getting introduced as the person in the field makes your job very much easier: instead of establishing authority all you have to do is not lose it!

## So what are the big takeaways here?

- **Prepare your physical environment before the audience arrives.** Have everything set up as you want it, such as the layout of the chairs, handouts as people come in, pens for note-taking etc.
- **Act as though you expect a certain behaviour from your audience.** No matter how badly you might be shaking inside, act with confidence. Fake it if necessary – your audience can only respond to what they see, not what you're feeling inside.
- **Establish your authority immediately and directly.** For example, you could show your audience your research (just a pile of work will do, don't go over the research itself) or even just state, matter-of-factly, that you've been working in this area for five years.

## Sources

Zimbardo, Philip, *The Lucifer Effect – Understanding how good people turn evil* (Random House, New York, 2007)

Milgram, S. (1963), 'Behavioral Study of obedience', *The Journal of Abnormal Psychology*, Vol. 67 No. 4 pp 371–8

## See also

Chapters 13 and 25 – It isn't just physical circumstances that influence how people behave: see **Being who you are** and **Blaming the right people**

Chapter 21 – The so-called 'Nudge Unit' has some interesting things to say about getting people to behave in the 'correct' ways. See **Being more persuasive**

## Further reading

Philip Zimbardo – who wrote *The Lucifer Effect* and ran the original experiments – has a handy website at: http://www.zimbardo.com. It's not particularly pretty but it does have some handy links to start you off.

The website for the actual experiment itself is at: http://www.prisonexp.org. It's not pretty – either aesthetically or in terms of what it says about people.

Dr Zimbardo has been involved in a lot of research other than his prison experiment, including looking at what went wrong at Abu Ghraib prison in Iraq. He talks about it here: http://www.ted.com/talks/philip_zimbardo_on_the_psychology_of_evil. A note of caution: be aware that it contains some horrible images.

The concept of the 'Illusion of Control' suggests that we are all less self-controlling than we like to think and that the circumstances in which we find ourselves have a lot more to do with who we are and how we behave than we realize or admit. A good starting point is the wikipedia entry at: http://en.wikipedia.org/wiki/Illusion_of_control

# 24 THE BEST OF POWERPOINT®

*How good do you have to be to be better than the rest?*

I'm sure you'll have heard the joke about two men suddenly faced with a large lion, clearly dangerous and hungry. One of them immediately puts on his running shoes and prepares to make a dash for it, despite his terror. With gallows humour his companion mocks, saying: 'You can't be serious! You're not going to outrun a lion!' to which the runner replies, calmly: 'I don't need to be faster than the lion. I just need to be faster than you.' (Yes, I know! I've used that joke earlier. Deal with it.)

How good does your presentation need to be to stand out from the crowd? That's the topic of a revelatory paper published in 2012 by a mixed bunch of researchers – two from different parts of Stanford University, one from Harvard and one from the University of Amsterdam. Kosslyn and his co-authors devised eight psychological principles for a good PowerPoint® slide deck: I talk about the various principles elsewhere in this book, so for now I'm going to go over them only briefly, because what's really important is how well the slide decks they looked at actually stuck to those principles. (We can effectively consider these principles as a form of best practice.) The table below gives a very simplified overview of the principles.

What Kosslyn and co. then did was to:

- create a five-fold categorization of presentation topics (education, business, etc.)
- use Google to look for online PowerPoint® files
- select these files at random from the first ten pages of Google results
- assess them for how often these broke their ideals of best practice.

| Which part of the process is involved? | The name of the principle | How it might look when it's applied |
|---|---|---|
| Encoding the information – that is, making initial sense of it, using our eyes, ears and so on | Discriminability | Type needs to be big enough and words, etc. need to be separated sufficiently to make reading them easy |
| | | Foreground and background colours need to be suitably different |
| | | Lines in shading should be angled at at least 30 degrees to be easily distinguished |
| | Perceptual organization | Labels on a figure should be closest to the item that they relate to |
| | | Colour can be used to group things, even if they're physically separate on the page |
| | | Things that *aren't* related should be shown in ways that don't allow people to artificially bunch them together |
| | Salience | Movement attracts attention, so animations should be used appropriately |
| | | Visual disparity draws attention – such as an 'exploded' wedge in a pie chart |
| Working memory – that is, making sense of the information we've perceived | Limited capacity | Information should be provided only at the rate the audience can handle it |
| | Informative change | People expect change to mean something, so pointless changes (such as in fonts or shifting from calling something a 'bird' to a 'fowl') is confusing |

(*Continued*)

| Which part of the process is involved? | The name of the principle | How it might look when it's applied |
|---|---|---|
| Encoding to long-term memory – that is, putting in some kind of framework and setting it up to be recalled as necessary later | Appropriate knowledge | People can only make sense of information if they have the necessary starting information; for example, using terminology that isn't already known makes things harder (jargon, anyone?) |
| | Compatibility | It's easier to make sense of things if the way it is presented matches with what is being presented – for example it's easier to read the word 'red' if it is displayed in red colouring than if displayed in blue |
| | Relevance | People generally find it easier to make sense of things if the right amount of information is given |

The way the files were assessed worked like this. In the first instance, two people (who were checked to make sure they pretty much agreed with each other) scored the files and gave them a score of zero if the file was good, or a one if it broke even one of the principles. Two more assessors repeated the process in a more lenient style. The good news is this — you don't need to be particularly good to score better than a typical online PowerPoint® deck. In fact, an average walking pace is all you need to be safe from the lion! Even at the better end of the spectrum, the principle of compatibility was broken only 31 per cent of the time but by contrast the principles

The researchers only looked for files with the familiar .ppt ending. They didn't include the newer .pptx or Apple Keynote®'s .key ending because, they felt, people using these types of file weren't representative of the general population of PowerPoint® users. They also limited the slide-decks to between 15 and 100 actual slides. (On a personal note, I tend to lose the will to live well before the 100th slide.)

of discriminability and limited capacity were broken in pretty much every single example, even in the liberal marking scheme.

What this means for you as a presenter is that it's not hard to get yourself a reputation as a great one. A little effort to think about whether you're giving people enough information; and giving it at the right pace; using large enough text in a sensible font; and so on, and you're going to be considerably better than the rest.

Of course, all of this might not matter if people don't care about these principles being broken, so Kosslyn and co. carried out an anonymous online survey about how often volunteers (who might not be representative of everyone who sits through presentations) felt the principles were broken and, very importantly, how annoyed they were when this happened. The results were no surprise to me when I read them: all the principles that could be tested were broken a lot of the time and each of them annoyed the audience to some extent or another.

From a presenter's point of view, what you should do with this information is pretty clear, once you know which principle was broken the most... it was limited capacity. In other words, far too many slides held far too much information so that people couldn't handle the data, and certainly couldn't handle it before the next slide appeared. Another bugbear turned out to be presenters who read the slides. And on the basis of open questions in the survey, things like not knowing how to work your equipment annoys people very much, as does not knowing the slides well, in advance of delivering from them and not being set up before your audience arrive.

As the paper puts it, summarizing the respondents: 'Don't waste my time! If you're not going to properly prepare then just send me a memo with information instead!'

And if you need me to spell out for you how to make your presentation better than the others, after you've read all that... well you need more help than a simple, short book is going to provide.

Finally, of course, it's worth mentioning something the paper itself finishes with – even if you don't break any of the principles it doesn't mean your presentation will be any good. You can still deliver a presentation that looks good in terms of this kind of analysis but fails by others – not least because as the authors are at pains to point out, all they did was look at the slides... the presenters themselves are a whole different can of worms.

## So what are the big takeaways here?

- **Think about things from your audience's point of view and make sure you provide them with the information they need and only the information they need.** Present it as slowly as they need it.
- **Hide your 'working out'.** That is, be ready before they arrive, check that everything works and that you know how to use it. To make sure you cover everything, I suggest making a checklist of the things you'd need to check well in advance of the presentation, since in the heat of the moment you'll forget things. (Trust me on this, this is experience talking.) Murphy's Law states that whatever *can* go wrong *will* go wrong and it's your job as a presenter to stop this from happening.
- **Don't overload your slides with either too much information or too much animated movement.** Clarity lies at the heart of sparsity. Make sure that, as far as you can, what you have to say is matched by the way you say it.

## Source

Kosslyn, S. M., Kievit, R. A., Russell, A. G. & Shephard, J. M. (2012), 'PowerPoint® presentation flaws and failures: a psychological analysis', *Frontiers in Psychology*, Vol. 3 Article 230

## See also

Chapter 19 – See **Doctors know best** to look at how things can be designed to help audiences learn in other ways

Chapter 38 – To explore what fonts to use on screen, sticking to these principles, see ☞ ⌂♞❄♦

## Further reading

You don't have to be great: just better than the others. With my tongue firmly in my cheek, see: https://kerricox.files.wordpress.com/2012/04/outrun-the-bear.jpg

*Is your audience affected by active or passive descriptions?*

I don't know if you remember the fuss, but back in 2004, the US Super Bowl had some half-time entertainment from Justin Timberlake and Janet Jackson. You're not likely to remember that, I suppose, except that at the end of the dance routine, something went wrong and Janet Jackson's breast was exposed to the audience – live, on national television. I don't expect anyone who was actually there saw all that much. Truth be told, even the television recording is too blurry to be of much interest.

The question of whose fault it was became a big legal (and therefore financial) question – and it was a question looked into in a series of experiments from two researchers at Stanford University, California. Fausey and Boroditsky were interested in whether or not 'linguistic framing' can 'shape construal even for well-known events'. (The word 'construal' here is the psychologists' term for how people perceive, comprehend and interpret the world, and in particularly the behaviour of other people in relation to themselves: my defining example is to look at what responses people have to a smaller (or bigger) birthday present than they think they 'should' have got.)

In the first of these experiments a group of students was asked to read one of two short descriptions of an accident in a restaurant where Mrs Smith (who seems to be related to television's Mr Bean) accidentally set fire first to her napkin, then the tablecloth and then the carpet. Two questions followed – the first asked how much Mrs Smith was to blame and the second asked how much Mrs Smith should pay the restaurant. The important difference between the two descriptions lay in whether, simply put, Mrs Smith was named as an active 'agent' of the incident or not. For example: 'she flopped her napkin on the centrepiece candle' compared to 'her napkin flopped on the centrepiece candle'. In the terminology of the paper, these are called agentive accounts and 'non-agentive' accounts, for obvious reasons.

When you read the agentive account, it has absolutely almost no statement of guilt – certainly not malice: in fact the way it was written made it pretty clear to me when I read it that the whole affair was an accident and all Mrs Smith could be accused of was clinical clumsiness. Despite this, participants who read the agentive account attributed more blame and wanted to impose higher levels of blame and greater penalties compared to people who read the non-agentive account.

From a presenter's point of view, the main application here is simple: use 'agentive' phrases. You can do this, for example, by using names and *active* descriptions. You'll have more impact on your audience if you use clear, 'agentive' phrasing such as 'We found that...' rather than 'It was found that...'.

In a different piece of research, published in 2011, Fausey and Boroditsky looked at the idea of 'passive language' in an innovative piece of research using people who spoke different languages. English tends to be a very 'agentive' language and we might say something like 'I broke the vase, but it was an accident' whereas other languages, such as Spanish, would use phrasing that translates more like 'The vase broke itself'. They showed a series of videos where things like pencils were broken on purpose and by accident, and asked monoglot native speakers of English and Spanish about what they'd seen. The results were interesting: when there was a deliberate act, both groups remembered things as well as each other, but when it came to the

Being scientists, Fausey and Boroditsky weren't content to let things go at this point and so they conducted a second experiment, this time also giving people information about Mrs Smith's culpability according to a panel of experts. Sure enough, participants were influenced by the apparently objective information, but they continued to be influenced by the agentive-vs-non-agentive aspects of the experiment. The two influencing factors of the way the description was written and the opinion of experts both had an effect but an independent effect.

accidents, the English-speaking participants were much better at recalling who'd done what. In other words, the more active the descriptions and the way we think, the better our chances of remembering them. How we speak, as presenters, is fundamentally important to our audience's chances of remembering what we tell them.

> Presenters can pretty easily use this kind of information, too, simply by providing their audiences with information gleaned from independent sources – that is, by using sources other than you, the speaker.

Use active phrasing. It would appear that passive sentences result in a lower.... no, stop it!

Going back to the original research, there's another question to be addressed – whether or not people are still affected by agentive descriptions when they were being told about something that wasn't new to them... enter, if you'll pardon the pun, Janet Jackson's breast.

Taking their research a logical step forward, Fausey and Boroditsky carried out a study in which participants:

- read about the famous 'wardrobe malfunction' (only)
- read about it and then watched the video
- watched the video and then read about it.

In short, the way the description was framed (as either agentive or non-agentive) was important to who got blamed (Janet Jackson, Justin Timberlake, or luck) and by how much. Not only that, but the framing even affected the hypothetical amount of a fine for the broadcasting company (CBS). What's more, the effect of the way the description was framed seemed to be biggest if participants read the description before they saw the video, and was even more if they didn't see the video at all and had only the description to go on!

There are a couple of interesting things we can use when we're making presentations that come out of this. First, the way we describe things, actively or passively, really, *really* matters.

We need to make sure our descriptions are active and clear. Audiences don't like passive material – ask any politician as they try to avoid saying things like 'I made a mistake' by substituting what sound like weasel-worded denials of the type 'mistakes were made'!

But the second thing that presenters can do goes perhaps one step further than the original research intended to do. (That said, it's certainly something I've noticed myself as I've trained people and it's a commonly held belief among other trainers I talk to.) It's worth considering telling people what they're to look for before you give them the evidence: certainly the research here suggests that the video evidence didn't change people's minds, once they'd read the agentive description. What's more, we know from lots of other work that people tend to interpret evidence in ways that support their prior beliefs (you know it's true, just try having any political argument around the family dinner table where no one can quite deliver the knockout blow) so it could easily be that having once decided that, for example, Justin Timberlake was responsible for exposing Janet Jackson, the way they viewed the video subsequently was anything but objective – they saw what they had already decided they were going to see. For more on this, see the chapter entitled **First things first**.

Feel free to watch the video yourself and make up your own mind.

Here's one final thought. In 2010 another piece of research, this time by Danziger and Ward, looked into how bilingual people reacted to descriptions in the two languages they spoke. You might not be surprised to know that there was a pretty clear bias in how people responded to things, depending on whether descriptions were in their own language or not. It's a bit of a stretch to say that you should only speak to people in their own language (or if you're only speaking to people in your home country speak to people in their own accent) but it could have implications for how people react when you use jargon and slang that they don't find familiar...

## So what are the big takeaways here?

- **Use active, agentive descriptions when you're explaining who did what.** Use active phrasing and be very clear about things. Don't say 'the overspend was done by Fred'; instead say 'Fred overspent'.
- **Before you provide evidence,** such as a video, or perhaps even data presented in a graph, tell your audience what you expect them to be able to see, in order to make them more likely to see it.
- **Consider cultural differences.** People whose thought processes aren't as person-centric as English speakers will probably see things in a different way. Make sure you don't make implicit assumptions that everyone thinks the way you do. It might not even need to be something as radical as using a different language – even a business's culture can have the same effect of defaulting either to looking for problems in the system, or looking for mistakes made by people.

## Sources

Fausey, C. M. & Boroditsky, L. (2010), 'Subtle linguistic cues influence perceived blame and financial liability' *Psychonomic Bulletin & Review*, Vol. 17 No. 5 pp 644–50

Fausey, C. M. & Boroditsky, L. (2011), 'Who dunnit? Cross-linguistic differences in eye-witness memory', *Psychonomic Bulletin & Review*, Vol. 18 pp 150–7

## See also

Chapters 23, 22, and 13 – For more on how people can be 'led' by others and influenced by conditions, see **The Lucifer Effect** and (briefly!) **And more persuasive still** as well as **Being who you are**

Chapter 35 – To look at the opposite of seeing what we're told is there, look at **Blindness isn't in the eyes** and see what we don't see that really is there

## Further reading

Try Googling 'Janet Jackson costume malfunction' for the infamous Super Bowl video

This handout – from part of the University of Washington – is a really handy little aide-mémoire with the bonus of other notes, too: http://www.bothell.washington.edu/getattachment/wacc/resources/handouts/handoutactivepassive-1.pdf

# 26 IT'S GRIM UP NORTH

*Does your accent affect how your audiences react?*

You'd not know it from the way I speak, but I was born in Sheffield (which likes to think of itself as a northern town but is really just the north-Midlands) and I'm an adopted Geordie. I love the Geordie accent, but I do recognize it can be a little difficult for people to understand who aren't lucky enough to live there. Geordie is more like Norwegian than English in many ways: in fact I can remember a friend of mine telling me that while drinking in a Norwegian bar he stood up and said: 'H'way; am gan yam' and the locals all said goodnight. (For those of you who can't read Geordie, that means 'Right then, I'm going home'.)

The thing is, the accent we use in our presentations might have quite a strong impact on how our audience responds to us. Anecdotal stories abound about companies putting their call centres in certain parts of the UK to make use of accents that are trusted more than others. But anecdotes aren't data, so a bit of research is called for, and it's not hard to find. (In fact, it was a topic for debate even at the very first International Conference in this subject area back in the late nineties, held in the UK[1].) One of the most striking papers[2] is from three researchers from the University of Notre Dame, Indiana, in the US.

Their first experiment was simple. College students listened to a taped description of what the researchers called a 'difficult-to-describe' colour. (In my case this might include anything other than simple primaries and a couple of shades of grey as anyone who's been shopping with me well knows.) In fact, that difficult-to-describe-ness was what they were told the experiment was about – and half of them were also told there had been technical problems with the recording. In fact, for these people occasional bursts of white noise were superimposed onto the tape, making it harder for them to figure out what was going on.

After the experiment the participants were asked to name the colour described, and to no one's surprise, there was a statistically significant difference in success rate between the two groups, in favour of those who listened to the unadulterated tape. However, a whole batch of other questions revealed some more interesting reactions. Compared to the unadulterated tape, people who listened to the tape with white noise bursts on it also described the speaker as:

- of lower status
- less trustworthy and friendly
- of a lower social class.

None of these things could possibly be reliably inferred from a bad bit of recording, any more than hair colour can, and yet they were, along with a few other things – all of which suggests people infer far more than can possibly be justified.

From a presenter's perspective the lesson is clear: background noises that make you harder to hear and understand will reduce your audience's perception of you in ways that are perhaps unreasonable and certainly very unfortunate. My approach is to make a point of consciously looking around before a presentation for things that might cause background noise, and doing whatever I can to mitigate those things. Closing windows isn't rocket science, politely asking the people next door if they wouldn't mind not leaving their office door open takes no real effort. The trick lies in remembering to do it. (My approach is to include this kind of thing on a checklist to run through before I start – so simple!)

Not content with looking at irritating noises cutting in, the research went a bit further. In a second experiment, 90 students were involved, and listened to colour descriptions as before – but this time with more variations. Three recordings were made by 'male speakers of Standard English' and a further three by 'male speakers of Spanish-accented English'. For each of these options, two more variations were made, one with long, continuous elements of white noise and one with shorter bursts. That gives 18 variations in total.

As you might expect, in recordings with bursts of white noise, the accuracy of picking the right colour goes down and things go from bad to worse for recordings with a continuous blast of white noise. What's more, the results for questions assessing the social status of the speaker fall even further – which is remarkable, given that the noise clearly has nothing to do with the speaker and his social status.

However, when you compare the scores for the Standard English speaker with the accented English speaker, the results are a little depressing: accented speakers were marked more negatively for quite a number of the personality and social dimensions – status, social class and so on. What's more, the effect of the white noise was markedly stronger in many ways on the perception of the accented speaker than the non-accented speaker.

As presenters it might be difficult to modify our accents – particularly in the short term – but what we can certainly do is make reasonable efforts to make things easier for our audience. For example, this research suggests it's a

> If you're unconvinced that we don't notice our own accent, think about the times someone has played you a recording of yourself... Does the recording sound like you expected it to?

very good idea to make considerable efforts to speak clearly. Unfortunately, what sounds clear to us, doesn't always sound so clear to our audiences. Not only are we used to the sounds of our own voice (and therefore don't hear our own accents) but we know, and have thought through, what we're saying... audiences don't have that luxury of having heard repeatedly what we're saying (as we design and rehearse our presentations); they only get the one stab at it.

One particularly handy way of making yourself easier to understand before you start your presentation is to warm up your face, and mouth in particular. There are any number of warm-up exercises scattered all over the web, so feel free to Google to your heart's content. However, one that I've found to be very effective is simply to yawn (in a way that feels like I'm about to dislocate my jaw, not the polite, behind-the-hand type of yawn) and to rub my face with both hands. As a clean-shaven man (at the moment), the area I rub is the area I shave; for women (or bearded men!) it's the same parts of the face. Because English is a very heavily articulated language, pay particular attention to your top lip as warming it up can make a lot of difference.

Think of it like this. You'd not play a sport without warming up the appropriate muscles first, so why would you try to speak to an audience without similarly warming up your appropriate muscles? If you've got a little more time than is needed for the simple yawn-and-rub, try running through a couple of these tongue-twisters:

- Mary Mac's mother's making Mary Mac marry me,
  and my mother's making me marry Mary Mac.
  I need to marry Mary to get Mary to take care of me,
  and we'll all be making merry when I marry Mary Mac!
- Knives and forks and spoons and pudding and knives and forks and pudding (repeated)
- The lips and teeth and the tip of your tongue (repeated).

As a personal aside to finish off with, I find it helps to imagine you're making your presentation to a slightly deaf, very posh, maiden aunt from the south of England; the type who gives you cucumber sandwiches with the crusts cut off. Speak as though you're desperately trying to impress her, so you remain written in her will and benefit from her fortune…

## So what are the big takeaways here?

- **Do everything you possibly can to remove background noise.** That might sound obvious, but you'd be amazed at the number of times I've been asked to give a presentation while the venue staff cleared up the teacups!
- **Make a conscious and concerted effort to speak clearly.** You'll need to work a lot harder than you think you will, because all your natural day-to-day practice at speaking will be with your natural accent. What sounds 'overdone' to you will probably sound fine to your audience.

- **Warm up your lips and face before you begin your presentation**. Find somewhere away from your audience and stretch your facial muscles.

## Sources

1 Giles, H., Robinson, W. P. & Smith, P. (Eds), *Language: Social Psychological Perspectives*, Selected papers from the first international conference on social psychology and language held at the University of Bristol, England, July 1979 (Pergamon, Oxford, 1980)

2 Sebastian, R. J., Ryan, E. B., Keogh, T. F. & Schmidt, A. C. (1980), 'The Effects of Negative Affect Arousal on Reactions to Speakers' in the above book

## See also

Chapter 5 – It's not just how you pronounce things, it's how fast you speak: see **Fast and hard**

Chapter 29 – Background noise is one thing – background music is another: **Put a record on**

Chapter 31 – Have a look at **Being judged** for an idea of how people judge you on the way you look, rather than on how you sound

## Further reading

If you want to find out what different accents sound like, you can try the British Library's survey of English accents at http://sounds.bl.uk/Accents-and-dialects/Survey-of-English-dialects

There's more work on how accent affects credibility at http://psychology.uchicago.edu/people/faculty/LevAriKeysar.pdf

On the other hand, there's a counter-paper here: http://mindmodeling.org/cogsci2013/papers/0258/paper0258.pdf

In 2013, ITV's *Tonight* programme ran a survey of 4,000 people to gauge their reactions to UK accents. A bit of a hyped-up write-up can be found at http://www.itv.com/news/2013-09-25/28-of-britons-feel-discriminated-against-due-to-accent. (Note that I've no way of knowing how well run the survey was!)

A good place to start with working on your voice is Stewart Pearce's *The Alchemy of Voice* (Hodder & Stoughton, London, 2005). My own copy is battered from use.

# 27 FASHIONABLE FEAR

*Can we simply wish away the nerves of making presentations?*

In a thorough and elegantly accessible piece of research, Alison Wood Brooks of the Harvard Business School looks at how we can take away the fear of presenting, simply by reframing it – that is, by doing something as simple as giving it a different label.

There's a lot we know about nerves when it comes to making presentations. For example, when people feel anxious prior to an important task such as making a presentation (or even during that task), it impairs their performance – specifically by reducing working memory and decreasing self-confidence, etc. The problem, of course, is that it's very difficult to do anything about this problem because anxiety is an automatic response: it's not something our bodies are in control of, any more than we can control if we shiver when we're cold or sweat when we're hot. Some of the research that Wood Brooks builds upon points out that trying to hide or suppress anxiety is both difficult and ineffective.

It might be worse than ineffective, in fact, and it might be downright counter-productive, as *pretending* to ourselves that we're relaxed when our bodies *know* we aren't takes up energy and effort. This mental capacity is better spent on doing the thing that's making us anxious in the first place... such as delivering a presentation. Nothing in science is ever that simple of course, and there's some contrary evidence

> The whole thing is a little more complicated, of course, because of the difference between 'trait anxiety' (which is to do with long-term issues) and 'state anxiety' (which is the result of a specific stimulus, such as an exam or a public performance).

that some levels of anxiety can be performance-enhancing at certain times (for example, a low level of anxiety can give us the motivation we need to carry on working when we'd rather stop).

Part of the issue, Wood Brooks argues, is that trying to convince ourselves that we're feeling calm is asking too much – we're trying to change from a high-energy state to a low-energy one. What if, she asks, we tried something more subtle instead, and shifted from one high-energy state (anxious) to another, similarly high-energy state (excited)? Would that be easier – and perhaps more successful? The terminology she uses is 'arousal congruent'. In an annoying irony, convincing ourselves to make a shift between states that are not arousal congruent isn't going to help because the effort of doing so cancels out any benefit the end product might give us.

As an interesting aside, before rushing into her experiments, Wood Brooks carried out a simple test of lay beliefs, to see if she was right in her assumption that people thought advice to 'calm down' was the best way to deal with an upcoming keynote presentation.

Reassuringly, people did. Overwhelmingly. More than 90 per cent of people thought the best way to handle an upcoming presentation was to 'try to calm down' – and furthermore, there was no difference in this opinion for different ages, genders – or how much experience people had already got as a public speaker.

After that, there are three big experiments.

In study one, 113 English-speaking students (with an average age of 20) were randomly split into three groups and told they were to sing, in front of each other, using a karaoke game. The game's software was used to measure how well they'd sung, based upon things like volume, pitch and note duration. To hype things up even more, participants got paid (a little) more if they did well. The research bit here is that the three groups, otherwise identical, were told to say to themselves:

- 'I am anxious'
- 'I am excited'
- or to say nothing at all.

As well as the software's measure of how well people had sung, they were to rate how excited they were. The long and the short of it is that the second group in the list above reported themselves as being more excited but – importantly – the karaoke software also rated them as statistically significantly better performers. Those who said nothing came second and those who told themselves they were anxious came third. The results were not only significant but huge – with average scores ranging from a little over 80 per cent accurate down to about 52 per cent.

The application in the world of the presenter is self-evident since you can use this technique for handling your performance nerves. The second study is even more directly useful, though, because here public speaking was directly included.

This time 140 English speakers with a similar age profile to the first group were recruited, told to prepare a persuasive public speech about why they were a 'good work partner' and also told that they would be judged by a panel. Participants were split into two groups, who had to say to themselves:

- 'I am excited' or
- 'I am calm'.

The results were pretty incontrovertible. When they were rated by independent observers, the 'excited' group were thought to be:

- more persuasive
- more competent
- more confident
- more persistent.

The 'excited' group also spoke for longer and felt better about things, too. All in all, the results leave little to the imagination and it should be pretty obvious how you can use this research.

The third study had a similar set-up and looked at performance in a maths test, this time using 188 participants. Results were measured not only using the scores in the test, but also by monitoring the heart rates of participants and their subjective feelings. Without going into the statistics of it all, when you compare *rethinking* anxiety as calmness (or don't do anything at all) with *reframing* anxiety as excitement, the 'excited' people felt calmer and did better. Interestingly, though, there wasn't any effect on heart rates. This raises the tricky question of how the process of reframing anxiety of excitement works, but is consistent with the idea of arousal congruence.

Taking this question one step further, Wood Brooks finishes her paper with a look at mechanisms. Now, I have a confession here: I'm an empiricist – I spent two and a half decades as a research scientist looking at what happened, with precious little need to examine why it happened. Theories were great, but observed data wins every time if theory and data don't say the same things. What that means is that I read Wood Brooks' last experiment for two reasons only: because I'm nosey and curious; and because with this kind of research there's always the risk of the psychological equivalent of confusing two-times-two with two-plus-two. Both will give you the answer 'four' but it's not possible to generalize to other numbers, such as 3 or 13.

I was wrong to be so cynical.

Wood Brooks' experiment tries to examine the fact that simply saying to yourself that you're excited (rather than saying you're anxious or not saying anything at all) can have a positive effect on your performance. After all, it doesn't affect your heart rate (and by implication that's a proxy for a lot of physiological indicators). My initial thoughts – perhaps like yours – are that the effect we're looking at here links very clearly to Cialdini's principle of 'commitment and consistency' (*see* the **Being more persuasive** chapter) but Wood Brooks suggests that the effect is linked to shifting people's mindset from a 'threat mindset' to an 'opportunity mindset'.

There's a lot of work that suggests that people caught in a threat mindset see things more easily as a threat, and therefore don't perform as well as other people. Breaking out of that can be handy: for example, reframing a maths test as a challenge rather than a threat, or reminding people that stress is enhancing (rather than deteriorating) increases how well people perform in the test.

Sure enough, when the third study I've described was repeated, this time testing for a threat-vs-opportunity mindset, the 'excited' people scored higher. The implication is pretty clear. By looking at your presentation as an opportunity rather than as a threat you can improve the quality. The poet in me wants to leap to the observation that this improvement makes it more likely that you'll do well in your presentation and so the whole thing becomes a self-fulfilling prophecy.

## So what are the big takeaways here?

- **Before you make your presentation, say to yourself 'I am excited'.** Say it to the mirror, to an empty room or whatever you like, but say it.
- **Don't try too hard to fight the nerves by using techniques designed to calm you down.** It's too much mental effort to fight the arousal that comes with a performance. In any case, other research has shown that people think faster when they're aroused and calming yourself down too much might undo that effect.
- **Look for the positives that might come out of your presentation.** Personally, I suggest writing down a list of what can happen as a result of a good presentation, rather than just thinking about them. I find it more 'real' to see them than just to think them. Besides, if I just think them, all that happens is that I use up more brain-space trying to remember them.

## Source

Brooks, A. W. (2014), 'Get Excited: Reappraising Pre-Performance Anxiety as Excitement', *Journal of Experimental Psychology: General*, Vol. 143 No. 3 pp 1144-58

## See also

Chapter 7 – **Stand up! Stand up!** has other techniques for feeling confident

Chapters 36 and 18 – **Minding what you say** has more. And so does **Fit to talk?**

## Further reading

It's not just presenters who suffer from nerves. Here's a lovely little feature from a musician: http://www.bulletproofmusician. com/what-every-musician-ought-to-know-about-stage-fright

When you take a simple talk about how nerves work and add animations you get this five-minute video about nerves (the cells in the body, not the sensation of 'being nervous'): https://www. youtube.com/watch?v=uU_4uA6-zcE

The blog at *Psychology Today* can be a fascinating kicking-off point for all kinds of stuff. It's a bit of a rabbit hole, though, so be careful. A good starting point is with an article on the effects of emotions on the performance of athletes at: https://www. psychologytoday.com/blog/the-power-prime/201012/sports-the-power-emotions

Basically, when you're at the top of your game emotions are the big differentiator. Who knew?

# 28 STAY ALERT AT THE BACK

*For how long does your audience concentrate
(and do they actually)?*

Have you ever been so engrossed in doing something that you
forget about everything else? The task becomes so much the
focus of your attention you don't notice the passage of time; or
that you're getting hungry; or that you needed to stand up and
walk about before you got too stiff.

Psychologist Mihály Csíkszentmihályi has a term for that state:
he calls it being 'in flow' and it's the 'ideal' level of productivity/
engagement that results from working on something that is very
challenging while also having the skills necessary to carry out the
task. The figure gives a very simplified version of what's going
on: if there's an imbalance between the challenge and the level of
skill and things start to go wrong…

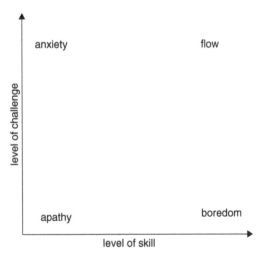

One of the great things about a presenter being in flow is that
time can pass without you noticing it – you're totally absorbed

in what you're doing – but one of the disadvantages is that this means you don't always realize that your audience isn't quite so fascinated. It undoubtedly will feel the passage of time.

So how long can your audience concentrate for?

There's a lot of tosh talked about this online and a lot of people making claims that, as a society, we now have an attention span equivalent to that of a goldfish. Fortunately, there's also some reasonable science. One of the more useful bits of research was carried out by looking at lectures in three different types of chemistry course, where three lecturers got students to report each time they realized they'd stopped concentrating by using a 'clicker'.

After two weeks of practice to make sure the system worked, data was collected for a month's worth of lectures in three courses, which included up to 186 students. I say 'up to' because there was no real way of checking which students had turned up for which lecture – the individual identities of the students were protected. Some of them will have turned up for all their lectures and others might have found other things to do with their time...

The classes were broken up naturally by the lecturers into 'teaching segments', some of which were the traditional 'chalk and talk' style (though with PowerPoint®) and other segments were demonstrations, practicals or other types of teaching that engaged students more actively than just by listening. This gave the researchers a chance to compare the different methods of giving information.

The idea was that every time a student realized they'd not been paying attention, they clicked one of three buttons to indicate if they'd been out of it for one minute, two to three minutes, or three to five minutes. (Presumably anyone who didn't pay attention for more than five minutes drifted off never to return.)

Now, there are all kinds of statistical niceties to be taken care of in a study like this to do with the fact that the number of clicks was counted in 30-second segments, and each lecture, lecturer and course tended to have different lengths of 'teaching segment'; and taking account of all of these means that the data are pretty stripped down by the time the actual analysis happens, but the results are potentially very important for presenters.

The thing is, the results pretty much blow away the old-fashioned ideas that people:

- concentrate more at the start of things and that the level of concentration goes down (in some pattern or other) as time goes by
- there's a firmly fixed concentration span of around 20 minutes.

Both of these ideas are pretty common and – to be fair – there's *some* evidence to support the idea that people have relatively fixed periods of concentration (but it's nearer 10 minutes than 20, if you require a single figure) but Bunce (the lead researcher) and her colleagues found something quite different.

They found that people started to report having lost concentration very quickly – with something of a peak in the first few minutes and a huge, statistically significant spike only five or so minutes in. It takes a real kind of special talent to bore people that quickly, so there must be something else going on. The question is 'what?' Looking at the pattern of clicks, it becomes pretty apparent that there's no single 'magic duration' for concentration during presentations: people phase in and out in cycles that are pretty hard to predict.

The ten-minute figure I just mentioned comes from the fact that all three different sets of lectures reported a statistically significant peak in clicks ten minutes into any given teaching segment, so if you want a single value, that's probably your best bet, but don't get too hung up on it.

> Incidentally, I've noticed since reading this research that my presentation segments average 12 minutes – although that was more from trial and error than wisdom – but it seems to work.

Something more straightforward that came out of the research that has huge implications for presenters is the relationship between how many clicks were reported compared to the type of pedagogic practice in the teaching segment involved. Remember that a teaching segment is one block using one style of delivery, so a 50-minute lecture/presentation that comprises a straightforward presentation followed by a practical demonstration, and then a discussion in groups and a quiz, then finally another straightforward 'teaching' section would count as four separate teaching segments. What this research found was pretty much what you'd expect: the number of clicks (representing a self-reported period of inattention) was statistically significantly lower in the teaching segments in which the students were actively involved.

In other words, being told things in a way that *allowed* people to disengage meant that they did – compared to when they were *required* to actively participate. Activity trumps passivity.

That's great of course, for those topics and audiences that lend themselves to the audience being actively involved, but there are times in any presenter's life when the presentation doesn't readily lend itself to that. Your topic might be trickier to deliver in that way, or the room layout might make it impossible, or (obviously) you might not feel your audience would be happy to go along with it. (I've just watched a cringe-making video of a speaker who got their audience to dance up on stage, for example.) In those circumstances you've got to make the best of what you've got.

But the research goes one huge, reassuring step further. There was a statistically significant drop in clicks between passive lecture segments that came before an active one, when it was compared to a similarly passive lecture segment which also followed an active segment. In other words, it looks like the effect of an activity is so strong that it can increase the amount of concentration your audience exhibits even into the next segment.

Now, I'm not suggesting anything as crude as presenters adopt an 'active presentations good; passive presentations bad' in an Orwellian style, but it's something to think about, isn't it?

So what we get from this research is that:

- audiences will zone in and out even from the very beginning of your presentation, but
- there is a peak of zoning out around the ten-minute mark
- these cycles-of-attention get shorter as the presentation goes on
- people pay more attention when they're actively doing something rather than passively listening, and
- the benefits of this increased attention roll over into subsequent parts of the presentation.

As a presenter, my personal take on doing this is that I try to structure any parts of my presentation that I expect to be the least engaging to go immediately after a higher-energy part, and that between segments I'm extremely bold and obvious in the way I reset the clock. Tricks I use are to do with things like:

- changing position on the stage (or get off it)
- changing medium (from slides to flip-chart, for example)
- changing slide design (colour schemes or the position of running headers)
- changing whether the audience looks at me or at handouts
- using black slides to signal the end of a segment.

## So what are the big takeaways here?

- **Remember that your audience won't be able to concentrate nearly as long as you can, once you're really into your presentation.** If in doubt, schedule breaks in your presentation to make you stop and think about whether to go on – perhaps adding a note to yourself on key slides. Think about trying to design your presentations in blocks of ten minutes or so. Be careful of being over-literal here, as some things need more than ten minutes to explain properly and other things need less, so treat this as a guideline, not a rule. In any case, there are lots of other mini-spikes in attention so it's not written, indelibly, in tablets of stone.
- **At the end of blocks, do something to 'reset the clock' of your audience's attention.**

- If it's appropriate (and possible), mix up segments of your presentation in which the audience is actively engaged compared to when you're 'just talking'.

## Source

Bunce, D. M., Flens, E. A. & Neiles, K. Y. (2010), 'How Long Can Students Pay Attention in Class? A Study of Student Attention Decline Using Clickers', *Journal of Chemical Education*, Vol. 87 No. 12 pp 1438–43

## See also

Chapter 4 – Pulling things from memory can help people believe what you're telling them. See **Repeating yourself**

Chapter 11 – Chopping around a bit can help your audience's concentration: see **Back to school**

## Further reading

Wikipedia is a dangerous place of shifting sands. Oftentimes it's full of wonderful stuff but sometimes you get sucked into what looks like something dreamed up as the love-child of George Orwell and Franz Kafka. This article on attention spans is a good starting point and at the very least it leads to interesting places: http://en.wikipedia.org/wiki/Attention_span

If you want to read something a bit more meaty about concentration spans, try this research from the University of Illinois: http://www.sciencedirect.com/science/article/pii/S0010027710002994

Going slightly sideways, we're often told that computer games are reducing our ability to concentrate. Even if we concede that is true, there are other benefits. You can start to explore them in a very accessible article from the BBC at: http://www.bbc.com/future/story/20130826-can-video-games-be-good-for-you

# 29 PUT A RECORD ON

*What's the effect of music in presentations?*

There's a lot of research going on here, as you can imagine. What's more, common sense and your personal experience is also going to suggest that music is important in your life and the way you think or feel about things. The chances are that you are listening to background music as you read this book. In modern life you're also 'subjected' to background music pretty much everywhere you go. For example, in the past few days alone:

- I've had background music on as I wrote bits of this book and did some of the research
- the supermarket played music as I shopped
- there was music playing in the lift as I went to a meeting (and as I came back from it)
- music played in the pub and restaurant as I relaxed with friends on Saturday.

Frankly, music is pretty much everywhere. In fact the only place I can almost guarantee no music is in the library, but looking around at how many other people are wearing headphones plugged into their phones, I suspect a lot of us prefer music to silence.

The emotional impact of music is taken as given in a lot of places. Imagine going to the cinema and listening to an action film with just the dialogue. Not only does the music have an emotional impact, it also tells us what emotion is appropriate. Towards the end of the film, when the good guys are apparently victorious and there's five minutes of the film left, the type of music played will tell us if we can relax or if the chief baddie is about to make a surprise reappearance, holding one of the goodies hostage with a knife to the neck.

Perhaps with so much music being used in our society, it's not surprising that there's a lot of research about it. And I do mean used, not 'played'. The next time you go into a restaurant, make a note of what kind of music they're playing: do they want you to relax and take your time, or are they into quick, profit-maximizing turnover?

Much of the research tends to focus on how we use music as individuals, too. When you're broken-hearted, what sort of music do you play and does it make you feel better (and if so, how – although there's less information about this last bit it seems)? That's pretty much the end of the good news, however. Frankly there's so much research it's almost impossible to make sense of it and find the common threads.

That said, there's some very interesting work being done on the effects of music.

## Music and learning

A few years ago there was a trend towards playing Mozart to children to make them smarter. CDs were sold to pregnant women, who were urged to play them to their unborn children so that they would be born with a higher IQ. The same music was to be played whenever the child was able to listen. Why Mozart? Good question. I've no definitive answer but I cynically suspect it might be something dreamed up by marketeers a long, long time ago and now accepted as one of those things that everyone-has-heard-of-so-no-one-asks-about.

The thing is, however, that the results of research into how effective this kind of thing is have been very mixed; but some researchers have found that playing background music to school pupils as they worked on maths tests had a positive effect, particularly among less able students.

## Music, physiology and emotion

Dopamine is a versatile and multi-functional hormone and neurotransmitter in our bodies. Inside the brain it can impact on everything from motor control, motivation, cognition and even how much we enjoy sex. (There are a lot of things dopamine does outside the brain too.) Getting a dopamine 'hit' is one of the reasons many of us find playing computer games so pleasurable – we're given a task, we achieve it and we get a dopamine/pleasure response as a consequence. That's similar to the real world, of course, except that in computer games, the cycle runs a lot more quickly and assuredly.

Back in 2011, some Canadian researchers [*see* Salimpoor et al, below] looked at how music could do the same thing. Music, they mused, is a pretty abstract thing… so how does it work? They got all high-tech, going so far as to use fMRI scans (a kind of MRI that looks at metabolism rather than anatomy) to look at what was going on inside people's heads as they listened to music (in a literal sense, not the metaphorical or psychological one). Sure enough, they found that dopamine hits could be released by music. Interestingly, they also found that a different set of routes in the brain lit up in their fMRI images for the anticipation and climax of music. As they so eloquently put it, given that dopamine is often referred to as a 'pleasure hormone', this set of results might 'help to explain why music is of such high value across all human societies'.

That's no small finding! And as presenters the implications are obvious.

## Music and recall

Pretty clearly there's an overlap here with how we react emotionally to things, and this very topic was taken up by researchers Michael Tesoriero and Nikki Sue Rickard at Monash University in Australia. They were interested in what they called 'the most informative framework to understand the effect of emotion-inducing music on the short-term recall of information about narratives'. What that meant in practice was that they took nearly 100 subjects and split them into four groups. Each group was played one of four types of music (happy, sad, fearful, calm) and then each group listened to a narrative. The narratives centred around different kinds of emotion, too.

The results were interesting. Their subjects were asked what they could remember of the narrative a short time later – and here's the interesting part – there was an association between the kind of information people could remember and the kind of music they'd been listening to. In other words, people who had been listening to happy music could recall more positive information when tested.

Let's not go overboard here, because we're only talking about short-term recall, but it does suggest that music can be a handy tool for presenters, to help them increase the amount and type of information that their audiences can remember, simply by using appropriate music at key moments.

Meta-research is research based upon rounding up the findings of other research (in a sense, it's what this book is doing) and three German researchers, led by Juliane Kämpfe (interestingly based in a physics department but researching psychology) have been doing just that. Background music, they observe, seems to have no effect on what people can recall (overall), but this is an average result, caused by several different effects cancelling each other out. They have some interesting comments to make:

- music, when compared to no music, seems to disturb readers and reduces memory, but it boosts emotional reactions;
- slower music vs faster music shows that the tempo (speed) of the music has an effect on how fast the listener carries out activities.

There are some interesting implications here for background music associated with tasks that you give your audience during your presentation!

| When and how to use music | Advantages of this approach | Disadvantages of this approach |
|---|---|---|
| Before the presentation starts, as your audience is coming in | It sets the scene and puts your audience in the right frame of mind for what you're going to say. | It's very blatant and if your audience isn't mentally in the right place, it could annoy it to the point of resenting you and your presentation. This seems to be particularly an issue if the audience don't want to be there and you're going to be giving a positive presentation, for example (motivational speakers, take note!). |
| When you give your audience something to do, or talk about. | Background music can also help break the ice here, as there's often a problem with audiences being inhibited and individuals not wanting to be the first person to talk. | It's technically tricky – and I recommend having music embedded in your slides to make things slicker. There's also the issue that some research has found background music can inhibit how clearly some people think, even though it might help other people. |
| As the audience leaves. | It's less blatant than playing music beforehand, and can help avoid the anti-climax that may hit people after you've finished. Milling around or shuffling out of a boardroom can suck the energy out of even the most inspired audience member. | It can feel a bit false if your audience spots what you're doing! |

I'd say it's impossible to generalize as all presentations are different, but speaking from a personal point of view there are a few options, not all of which are appropriate for everyone (obviously!).

With my scientist hat on, I wonder how a lot of these bits of research got around the Hawthorne effect. What's the Hawthorne effect? Bluntly, the Hawthorne effect is named after some (possibly apocryphal) research that found that there's a real problem with this kind of research, because the very act of researching how someone behaves can change how they behave. For example, if I'm sitting in the passenger seat of your car to observe how well you drive, the chances are you're not going to run any red lights (or at least I hope not). You might or might not run them if I'm not there – but the point is that I wouldn't know.

> If you find you want to use music in your presentations, either as background music or as a filler before you begin, you need to make sure that it's legal for you to do so. You can't just automatically play any old music you happen to have around and think it will work: the chances are you'll need a licence.

It's hard to imagine research that plays music to children while getting them to do some maths isn't similarly affected...

## So what are the big takeaways here?

- **Think carefully about if you want to use music and if so, how and where.** There's no doubt that music can be a scene-setter or mood-enhancer and if that's helpful to your presentation you could see about having music playing as your audience arrives (or leaves), for example.
- **It's probably a mistake to use background music during audience tasks in your presentation if you need them to concentrate on a difficult topic** (though it's fine for maintaining the energy levels in the room). For some people it helps but for others it gets in the way: the evidence suggests that smarter kids found background music less useful that less able school kids – and your audiences are bound to be smart, right?

- **Think carefully about licences – the fine for not having one is undoubtedly going to be greater than your fee for that presentation!** Check with your venue and ensure that you see a copy and follow their procedures – most venues with a licence will simply want to take a note of the artist and the name of the track that you use.

## Sources

Salimpoor, V. N., Benovoy, M., Larcher, K., Dagher, A. & Zatorre, R. J. (2011), 'Anatomically distinct dopamine release during anticipation and experience of peak emotion to music', *Nature Neuroscience*, Vol. 14 No. 2 pp 257–62

Tesoriero, M. & Rickard, N. S. (2012), 'Music-enhanced recall: An effect of mood congruence, emotion arousal or emotion function?', *Musicae Scientiae*, Vol. 16 No. 3 pp 340–56

Kämpfe, J., Sedlmeier, P. & Renkewitz, F. (2011), 'The impact of background music on adult listeners: A meta-analysis', *Psychology of Music*, Vol. 39 No. 4 pp 424–48

## See also

Chapter 26 – Music can be a form of background noise. For other distractions, see **It's grim up north**

## Further reading

Sue Hallam and Anastasia Kotsopoulou wrote 'The effects of background music on learning, performance and behaviour', which is freely available from the http://www.icanteach.co.uk looking at all the reasons we use and listen to music (there are three, in the end!).

Meanwhile, if you're in a mind for some even heavier-duty statistics, try Schäfer, Sedlmeier, Städtler and Huron's 'The psychological functions of music listening' published in *Frontiers in Psychology*, and which can be downloaded from: http://journal.frontiersin.org/article/10.3389/fpsyg.2013.00511/abstract

For a further summary of the effects of music (such as in shops and restaurants), have a look at this brief blog: http://www.businessinsider.com/effects-of-music-on-sales-2011-7?op=1&IR=T

# 30 WAVING NOT DROWNING

*But what should I do with my hands?*

I've just watched an otherwise great video where I was put off the content by the speaker's hands constantly flapping around. But only last week I watched a presentation where the speaker had his hands in his pockets, which didn't work either. So what to do with your hands for the best?

It's not a new question. As long ago as the mid-17th century there was advice being published [*see* Bulwer, below], using the fantastic word *chirologia* (meaning, apparently, the 'natural language of the hand'), which is still one of the influences in British Sign Language today. Nowadays, there are more books about body language than you can shake a stick at. Add to that the nonsense myth that only 7 per cent of meaning is conveyed in the words you say (which isn't supported by the research that it's attributed to [*see* Mehrabian, below]) and you can see the potential for big business.

But does all this hyperbole have any real substance? Or is it just a question of people feeling it's important – or even just wanting to make money?

Back in the late 1970s a trail of really interesting research started at the City University of New York. One of the researchers was interested in whether or not gesticulations actually added anything to the amount of understanding an audience had, over and above the spoken word. William Rogers (the researcher) was building on earlier work which went so far as to suggest that what you say and the gesticulations that go with it are so closely intertwined they're effectively one statement using two media. That means that gestures are part of the message. Rogers speculated that he could test this with a series of experiments: if he was right, comprehension should be higher if people can see the speaker, perhaps even when they can't see the speaker properly, such as if their mouth is obscured. What's more, 'visual advantage' will be greatest when conditions are least favourable in other ways too.

Rogers' starting point was a set of actions such as a car making a set of turns or a pigeon walking in a car park. Each of these actions was viewed for about 10 seconds by recruits who then described them to a second person while being recorded (after a bit of practice to get used to the process and the camera). After that, copies of the recording were manipulated by adding background white noise at various levels. Additionally, playback was sometimes done with the screen blacked out, so that you could hear things but not see them at all and, just to add to the complication, for some occasions when the recording was played back the TV used was adjusted (saturation and brightness) so that when you wanted it you could see the big gestures and so on but the faces/mouths of speakers were effectively obscured. It all sounds horribly complicated but what it meant was that there were some relatively natural descriptions of everyday events recorded and then played back to different people with the amount of visual information in full or reduced in a couple of ways (no faces/lips and nothing at all) and the amount of audio information reduced because of the background noise (at four different levels). In the jargon this mix of amount of audio information is called the signal-to-noise ratio, or SNR. Signal is what you want to hear, in this case the speech, and the noise is what you don't – in this case the white noise.

If Rogers was right, and gestures added to understanding, then comparing the full recording to the blacked-out recording – when only the audio was available – should give better results and, hopefully, the option with the faces blurred out but gestures visible would lie somewhere between the two. You'll be pleased to know that was exactly what he found. In other words, the more visual information you get along with the words, the more you understand. That said, some gestures were more important than others, naturally.

For presenters, the implications are clear. Not only is it important that people hear you, they need to see you. And while they can see you, you should gesticulate. I'm not advocating wild 'arm flapping' of course – that's movement not gesticulation – but simple, clean gestures can illustrate your point.

But Rogers also tested the effect of changing SNRs, remember? The first outcome is pretty obvious, that people understood more of what was said if they could hear clearly (a good SNR) but what followed is even more useful to presenters – the positive effect of gesticulations was more and more important to the audience as the SNR got worse. In other words, as presenters, we should make sure to remove as much background noise as possible, which is obvious, but it turns out we can at least partially compensate by using gestures as we speak.

Some years later, two researchers in Manchester [see Beattie and Shovelton, below] took this work further and differentiated between gestures which were made as though from the point of view of the subject of a story and gestures made from the point of view of a narrator. (They also found that even when people couldn't hear what was being said, they could understand up to about a fifth of what was intended if they could see good gesturing!).

As an aside, it appeared that gestures from the point of view of the protagonist in a story were related to transitive verbs (where there was an object to be acted on) and narrator-based gestures were associated with non-transitive verbs, generally to do with movement, travel or change etc.

For a presenter this can be remarkably useful as it gives a clear framework for what style of gesture or action you should make. If you're talking about movement or progress, gestures should be as a narrator but if you're describing a problem as 'a big one' that should be from the point of view of a protagonist (say looking up at something).

Their test suggested that gestures made from a character's point of view were generally more communicative than those generated from the narrator's viewpoint – about twice as informative, in fact. As a presenter, this means you might want to make sure you gesture as though you are involved in the story in some way. Obviously this is easier for some types of presentations than others (I can't imagine a gesture to indicate I'm a computer running tests very easily, for example) but my experience is that you don't need to be very literal in your gestures sometimes – a simple gesture made when you 'are' the computer is effective, so long as it's consistent. Obviously I make such gestures congruent with what I'm 'being' – a computer might be a small box shape with my hands, for example, not a huge T shape with my arms outstretched.

That idea brings me rather nicely to the process of creating gestures. Gestures need to be discrete, so that your audience can tell one movement from the next, because it's easier to interpret gestures if you know when they start and finish rather like it's easier to read words if you have spaces to show you where they start and finish.

A remarkably simple yet powerful way of creating these gestures is to adopt the approach used by experts in contemporary dance.

Rudolf von Laban created a (relatively) simple approach to understanding the how and what of movement [*see* Campana, below], a technique that is often used by both dancers and actors getting to grips with a character.

Laban suggested that for each movement you make, you should individually consider the following:

- space – in which direction should you move? Are you moving *to* something or *away* from it? Directly or indirectly?
- time – how quick should your movement be? Fast or slow? Or one then the other? What about sudden or smooth?
- weight – how 'heavy' should your gesture be? Is it a light movement or a heavy one?
- flow – is the gesture unfettered or limited in some way?

Obviously a full analysis of each and every gesture is probably overkill, but I've found personally that key elements of my presentations have been worth the effort of a few minutes of thought. Basically, this is because your audience will infer great meaning (potentially) from both the gesture you use, and the way you do it. For example, a gesture that starts slowly and feels heavy, finishing with a sudden stop will give an indication of either reluctance or some other form of resistance (such as the thing taking a lot of effort). Alternatively, a quick, throw-away gesture out to the side would give the impression of a trivial problem, dismissed easily.

On a personal note, I've found a guide written for teachers to help them with basic choreography for school pupils to be very helpful. The basic approach is to consider a key statement, and identify the key words within that. Once you've found them, identify an appropriate movement for that word, perhaps using the Laban technique or perhaps a more literal, physical representation. Then, whenever that key word is used, use the same gesture.

Now comes the critical part. When you're not making one of these key movements, don't move. You will, of course: everyone does. That's fine, because a series of isolated moves will look odd, but try to reduce it a little, so that your key moves stand out.

## So what are the big takeaways here?

- **Don't be afraid to gesture naturally as you talk,** particularly in situations when the audience might not be able to see you or hear you perfectly.
- **Consider whether your gestures should be from the point of view of a narrator or a character and use the most appropriate one.** When you have a choice, be a character.
- **Identify your key words and design a congruent gesture for them.** Keep those gestures for those key words – and those key words only – and, as far as you reasonably can, isolate them.

## Sources

Bulwer, John, *Chirologia: Or the Natural Language of the Hand and Chironomia: Or the Art of Manual Rhetoric* (Southern Illinois University Press, Carbondale, 1974)

Mehrabian, Albert, *Silent Messages: Implicit Communication of Emotions and Attitudes* (Wadsworth Publishing Company, Belmont, 1981)

Rogers, W. T. (1978), 'The Contribution of Kinesic Illustrators Toward the Comprehension of Verbal Behavior Within Utterances', *Human Communication Research*, Vol.5 Issue 1 pp 54–62

Beattie. G. & Shovelton. H. (2002), 'An experimental investigation of some properties of individual iconic gestures that mediate their communicative power', *British Journal of Psychology*, Vol. 93 Issue 2 pp 147–287

The best simple explanation I've found is in: Jillian Campana's 'Laban Movement Analysis: a tool for any actor' (2011)

## See also

Chapter 31 – To make the best impact and look the most credible, see **Being judged**

Chapter 13 – and **Being who you are**

## Further reading

TIN Arts (a dance company in the north of England) has written an interesting and accessible guide on creating shapes for dancers. The principles apply to gestures in your presentations, too. It's available from the website at: http://issuu.com/tinarts/docs/tin_arts_creative_movement_manual_-/0.

It's written for science teachers working with young children so don't feel obliged to try every technique but even a 'once-through reading' will probably suggest benefits to how you move when you speak.

To give you another starting point for how to make your gestures clear, try thinking of them as being the visual equivalent of an onomatopoeia. British Sign Language is a good starting point for getting you thinking the right way: http://www.british-sign.co.uk/british-sign-language/dictionary

# 31 BEING JUDGED

*How long is your honeymoon?*

It's hard to resist the famous old adage that 'you never get a second chance to make a first impression'. The big questions here are:

- how quickly are first impressions made?
- how important are those first impressions?
- how mutable are those impressions – or are they fixed in stone?
- what can I do to make a better first impression?

Unsurprisingly, there's big money to be made here. A quick Google search suggests somewhere in the region of a quarter of a billion web pages on the subject. And, of course, anything that pampers to our understandable paranoia is going to make someone, somewhere, some money. Fortunately, scientists aren't immune to being interested in this kind of thing and there's a steady stream of work looking at what it is about our faces that allow us to give a good first impression.

Looking at the second question first, the answer appears to be **very**. It's in bold for a reason. Back in 2005, a group of researchers reported their work looking at US Congressional elections over a number of years. Their results are rather depressing for anyone interested in politics with any kind of ideological hat on because it implies that the real issues aren't as important as we'd like to think. In short, the research suggested that people made a subjective assessment on the 'competence' of candidates they didn't know based on facial appearance (only). When that assessment was compared to how well the candidates actually did, they found that the more 'competent' candidate tended to gather more votes and get elected more often. (Other things, such as trustfulness and likeability didn't predict the outcomes – which perhaps says more about democracy in the United States than we'd like.)

All this from comparing black-and-white photographs of faces for only one second – and now we know how important the way you look is to how you're regarded.

Janine Willis and Alexander Todorov directly tackled the question of how quickly people judge people in a piece of research that I can only describe as fun and elegant. Working at Princeton University they used a database of amateur actors' photographs, dressed in grey T-shirts, with no beards, moustaches, earrings, glasses or visible make up, and showed these pictures to people, so that each picture was rated more than 40 times, on a nine-point scale, on whether the person was:

- attractive
- likeable
- competent
- honest or trustworthy
- extroverted/enthusiastic
- dependable/self-disciplined
- open to new experiences, etc.
- ambitious.

Some of these you might be able to infer from photographs, others clearly not. I don't know if you can tell I'm ambitious or not, for example, simply because I have grey hair and haven't shaved today…

There was no time limit on how long people took to do their scoring here, and these results were used as a baseline for later work. This later work consisted, simply, of showing various faces for 100 milliseconds, 500 milliseconds or 1,000 milliseconds and comparing the results of these evaluations with the baseline results with no time limits. The results were very clear: 'even after 100-ms exposure to a face, trait judgements were highly correlated with judgements made in the absence of time constraints'. In short, we make our minds up about things like how competent or trustworthy a person is after as little as a tenth of a second!

The implications are obvious: people have decided whether or not to trust you before you even open your mouth. That's handy for a presenter to know!

So what happens after that first, critical, fraction of a second? Not much, to be honest. Our opinions don't change over time – or at least not the time frame used in this research. What's more, even when people were given more time to make a judgement, they didn't really use it, making their decisions almost as quickly as when they had very little time. Two things did change over time however...

> An important aside here... from a presenter's perspective... is that the trait that most strongly correlated to the baseline measures wasn't attractiveness (which, let's face it, you can reasonably expect to judge immediately) but trustworthiness.

First, people simply became more confident about their initial judgements – and second those judgements tended to become slightly more negative. The definition of first impressions is pretty specific now – it's the immediate first impression of fractions of a second!

More work from Todorov (and others) managed to pin down fairly clearly and simply what it is that we use in those first critical thousandths of a second by using a combination of fairly advanced statistical analysis (Principal Components Analysis – PCA) and computer graphics. They created computer graphics of faces that they could manipulate, with various specific characteristics to investigate. This gave them data to perform a PCA to create what can be thought of as 'super-variables' (where groups of things are brought together on the basis of how well they relate to each other, statistically). For example, when looking at lots of measurements of the human body we might expect to find such a super-variable that includes height and weight, because they're generally reasonably closely related. In a form of 'statistical magic', the PCA process does this in a way that also tries to keep the super-variables as different as possible from each other at the same time. The result was only two super-variables that between them accounted for a little over four-fifths of the data.

The first of these was linked heavily to positives so that it was labelled 'trustworthiness' and the second was linked to measures of (for example) dominance, aggressiveness and confidence: it got labelled 'dominance'. And here things get really interesting, because in a set of further experiments, the authors found that:

• the dominance measure wasn't particularly sensitive to facial expressions; but
• the trustworthiness measure could be affected by the expression of the computer-generated face.

In other words, while the presenter can't do much about how dominant they appear by changing their expression, they can make themselves appear a little more trustworthy – for example, simply by smiling and so on.

Some of this is slightly depressing from a presenter's point of view, as there's not much we can do to change the overall way we look, short of plastic surgery – which might be taking things a little bit too far. Fortunately, some British work looked at using what it termed 'highly variable facial images'. Vernon and his colleagues point out that more or less all the work in this area is based upon single pictures of people: in real life, people move, have different expressions and change.

Building on the two 'super-variable' models, this work adds a third, called 'youthful-attractiveness', and with some equally complicated and clever statistical analysis, using 1,000 variable photographs (though all of Caucasian subjects to reduce one possible level of complexity) they figured out 'linear properties of objective facial attributes can be used to predict trait judgements with considerable accuracy'. In other words, there are things about how we look that we now know predict how people make their initial snap judgements.

Some of them can't easily be manipulated by presenters (surgery to increase the distance between your eyes, anyone?) but some of the others can. I've done a simple (and frankly partially subjective) bit of parsing in the table:

| Facial feature | What it affects | What you might be able to do about improving it |
|---|---|---|
| Orientation (front-profile) | Attractiveness | Make sure you face people as much as you reasonably can. |
| Head tilt | Attractiveness and approachability | Try to keep your head oriented so that your face is towards your audience – don't spend your time looking down at your notes or up over their heads at the back row. |
| Eyebrow area | Approachability and attractiveness (and dominance) | Reign in big, bushy and unsightly eyebrows. But don't overdo it, as you need good eyebrows to remain dominant. |
| Nose flare | Approachability | Don't do it – just don't. |
| Mouth area | Approachability and attractiveness (and dominance) | Smiling makes you more approachable and attractive. Don't do too much of it if you want to be seen as dominant. |
| Glasses | Attractiveness | If you don't need them, don't use them. |
| Beard or moustache | Attractiveness and dominance | No facial hair if you need to improve your attractiveness; but let it grow if you need to increase your dominance. |

Some of these are easier for men than women and vice versa, so take from it what you want!

## So what are the big takeaways here?

- **Smile and be positive.** And let the audience see your positivity and enthusiasm. Don't be too stand-offish. It makes you appear more untrustworthy.
- **Have a think about whether you need to increase how dominant you look to your audience, or how approachable you need to be.** That will be a combination of you and how you look and how you think of the audience. Then think about whether you want to make some changes to how you look to give a better first impression accordingly.
- It goes without saying, of course, but **make a big, focused and concerted effort to look your very best** when your audience first sees you.

## Sources

Todorov, A., Mandisodza, A. N., Goren, A. & Hall, C. C. (2005), 'Inferences of Competence from Faces Predict Election Outcomes, *Science*, Vol. 307 No. 5728 pp 1623–6

Willis, J. & Todorov, A. (2006), 'First Impressions. Making Up Your Mind After a 100-Ms Exposure to a Face'. *Psychological Science*, Vol. 17 No. 7 pp 592–8

Oosterhof. N. N. & Todorov. A. (2008), 'The functional basis of face evaluation', *Proceedings of the National Academy of Sciences of the United States of America*, Vol. 105 No. 32 pp 10087–92

Vernon, R. J. W., Sutherland, C. A. M., Young, A. W. & Hartley, T., (2004), 'Modeling first impressions from highly variable facial images', *Proceedings of the National Academy of Sciences of the United States of America*, Vol. 111 No. 32

## See also

Chapter 1 – First impressions aren't just for people; they're also for data. See **First things first**

Chapter 10 – Of course you can also give yourself a boost in the impression stakes by how you greet people: **Saying hello at the door**

Chapter 13 – Even before they meet you, people can be influenced. Getting introduced the right way is sometimes important. See **Being who you are**

Chapter 26 – In **It's grim up north** there's a discussion of how people judge you by your accent as well as by how you look

## Further reading

MIT has very recently released some work suggesting that we can pick up some visual information (such as identity) in as little as 13 milliseconds – it might be less, in fact, but the computer monitors the experimenters were using couldn't react any faster than that. See http://newsoffice.mit.edu/2014/in-the-blink-of-an-eye-0116 for a friendly write up.

Glasses and hair length get the research treatment at: http://onlinelibrary.wiley.com/doi/10.1111/j.1559-1816.1993.tb01064.x/abstract

If you're interested in how actors create their personal impact a good starting point is Patsy Rodenburg's 2008 book *The Second Circle: How to Use Positive Energy for Success in Every Situation*, published by W. W. Norton & Company. You can see her talking on YouTube too: https://www.youtube.com/watch?v=Ub27yeXKUTY

# 32 TELLING STORIES

*Should you use stories? And if so, how?*

Storytelling has been with us for as long as there have been people (probably). It's not new – in fact a couple of thousand years ago Aristotle wrote advice on how to tell a story: it should have a beginning, a middle and an end and should include a variety of realistic characters, some of whom suffer at least one reversal of fortune. Good advice.

There's a plethora of advice that says that stories are the way forward for presenting. Personally I'm not sure it's that easy if your presentation has to be entirely technical (though my experience is that few, if any, presentations should be like that) but for the majority of presentations it seems sensible. The problem is, it's almost impossible to carry out scientific research into the effects of storytelling on adults. (There's quite a bit about very young children but nothing that seems to translate sensibly into the world of business and so on.) How would you go about it? Give a presentation without a story, then give the same presentation with a badly told story and finally tell it again with a well told story? How would you measure the results? Count the yawns?

'Register' is the term storytellers use to describe how formal their style is. One of the most useful descriptions of register [*see* Montano-Harmon, below] suggests that there are five, ranging from the Static (for laws and so on that never change) to Formal, Consultative (the one we use in everyday speech), Casual (the way we speak to friends) and Intimate.

The idea is that you pick the appropriate one for your topic, audience and setting: getting it wrong can jar with your audience. It's probably okay to move from one register to one either side, but no leaps more than that.

And yet whole industries have been built on our human need for consuming stories. Imagine Hollywood without stories. Meanwhile people as pragmatic as the programme director of knowledge management at the World Bank have written excellent articles [*see* Denning, below] about the effectiveness of using stories in business, and a simple Google search for training in storytelling in London produced nearly nine million results. Even though most of these will be irrelevant, the sheer volume of interest is staggering – as is the money involved: one of the staple guides on the subject costs more than £60 in hardback.

Actually, this is a book with some great ideas in it; not least is a system for how you decide what kind of story you need to use in a four-step procedure based upon a number of points for each of three questions. (The fourth step is just to add up the points from the first three steps, so it's not hard!)

- First, think about the size of your audience and give yourself one point for an intimate group of two or so people; two points for a small meeting of several people with a good working history or relationship; three points for a formal meeting; and four points for a very structured setting such as a presentation.
- Second, ask yourself what you want your story to do. Give yourself a point if you want to connect with people; two points if you need to teach or explain something; three points if your teaching is really important and there is a key piece of information; four points if you're trying to entertain people.
- Third, reflect on the 'trigger' – that is, what it is that's making you pick a story. If you want to hear other people's thoughts, give yourself one point; count two points if you're responding to a sudden epiphany you've had; three points if you're responding to someone else's point or story; and finally four points if you're planting an idea or need to create a specific mood.

Add your points up and then decide what story to use on the basis that the fewer points you've given yourself the more personal the story needs to be. For up to six-ish points (inclusive) use a story of something that's happened to you. For six-ish points up to nine-ish use a personal story but this time it should be about someone else. Finally, for over nine-ish points use a story from some other background (or 'domain' in the jargon).

What that means is that if you're talking to accountants, use a story from a bunch of software engineers: if you're talking to NHS leaders, talk about racing drivers. (There's a famous story of how hospital procedures for critically ill children at Great Ormond Street were changed after two of the surgeons involved learned from Formula One pit stops. What's more, it's probably true!)

Stories have structure and short stories have to be very heavily structured – there's not much time in a presentation for the luxury of sub-plots or character development. A tool I like to use when I'm working on my own stories is to see if I can get them into a tweet. I can't, of course, but the discipline of trying to do that is handy. J. R. R. Tolkien's *The Hobbit* becomes: 'Hobbit helps dwarves get their home (and gold) back. Adventures abound, including finding a magic ring and killing a dragon'. A technique I've never fully mastered but which takes brevity even further is drawing my own cartoons – which is, essentially, a story and a comment on that story all in one. As a presenter, you can use that kind of thing very easily.

There is a particular problem for presenters as they *use stories* rather than just tell them. Storytellers tend to use detail to give authenticity but our audiences have neither the time nor the patience for that kind of detail. My personal approach is to get the audience to do some of the work, giving them only the necessary detail for them to create the pictures themselves. A few years ago I was introduced to the work of Ernest Hemingway, who is purportedly the creator of the shortest of short stories: a whole, emotion-packed narrative in six words, but where most of the 'action' takes place inside the readers' heads. It goes like this:

'For sale: baby shoes, never worn.'

To change tack slightly... Back in 1949, Joseph Campbell first published one of the seminal texts in the area of storytelling and identified a seven-step journey for heroes (or heroines) in stories.

As a presenter, you might need to cut short the hero's journey because of time constraints, but it's worth comparing your stories against what is now regarded by many as the definitive checklist to see how your stories stack up.

- Ordinary world – where you are at the start of things
- Call to adventure – something happens to change things
- Refusal of the call – a reluctance to get involved
- Meeting the mentor – getting some help from somewhere/ someone
- Crossing the threshold – deciding to move on to the quest and deal with whatever happened in the Call to adventure
- Tests, allies and enemies – the main thrust of the story, where the hero does things, usually unsuccessfully at first. Stakes often get raised here.
- Approach to the inmost cave – final preparations
- Ordeal – facing the consequences of failure
- Reward – when the ordeal is overcome
- The road back – the Call to adventure is reversed and the hero takes whatever he has gained back to the Ordinary world
- Resurrection – something's gone wrong and the Ordeal turns out not to be the end of things after all; another obstacle needs to be overcome (or the original Ordeal needs to be repeated)
- Return with the elixir – finally the hero gets back to the Ordinary world, but now things have changed.

For example, it's relatively easy to see, as a presenter, how a story of a restructure or other big organizational change can work in that storytelling structure. Just like *Star Wars*. I find it restricting to limit my stories to this structure too rigidly, but it's certainly a handy practice to create/find your story and then check it against this structure as a checklist. If the story isn't working or your audience is unaffected by it, it may be that it's missing one of the key components above – find out which and add it.

## So what are the big takeaways here?

- **Tell stories.** Make sure they're the right kind of story for your audience and your circumstances and make them believable. Don't confuse real with realistic: your audience needs the latter but not everything that's real is realistic.
- **Try to get your audience to do some of the emotional work to get them more engaged.** Questions are handy here, or exercises that help them map the story to their own experiences and circumstances.
- **Make sure your story is tightly structured.** Or to put it another way: if it's not structured, it's not a story, it's just you talking.

## Sources

Denning, S. (2004), 'Telling Tales', *Harvard Business Review*

Montano-Harmon, M. R. 'Developing English for Academic Purposes', California State University, Fullerton

Gargiulo, Terrence L., *The Strategic Use of Stories in Organizational Communication and Learning*, (Routledge, Abingdon, 2005)

Campbell, Joseph, *The Hero with a Thousand Faces* (Pantheon Books, New York, 1949)

## See also

Chapters 5 and 26 – **Fast and hard** looks at how the way you speak when you tell your stories affects things, as does the chapter **It's grim up north**

Chapter 6 – For a broader context on one technique for telling your stories: **It's not what you say, it's the way that you say it**

Chapter 16 – The chapter **Story time** looks more at how effective stories are in your presentations

# Further reading

Nancy Duarte's book *Resonate* (John Wiley & Sons, Hoboken, 2010) is subtitled 'present visual stories that transform audiences' and explores the structure of stories pretty thoroughly.

If you want something a bit more hardcore, try *Making Connections* by Renate Nummela Caine and Geoffrey Caine (Addison Wesley Longman Publishing Co., Boston, 2nd edition, 1995).

Frankly I'm not sure how to describe *Heart Seeds* (Beavers Pond Press, Edina Minnesota, 2003) by WindEagle and RainbowHawk, but it's a must-read for serious storytellers

# 33 LEARNING STYLES

*Is it us? Or is it them?*

Everyone is different. What that means, among other things, is that everyone learns differently. However, proponents of 'learning styles' point out that while we're all unique there are certainly patterns – in much the same way that there are things that all men tend to share and that all women don't for example. That's probably a bit simplistic, because very few people would demonstrate that learning styles are as clear cut as that (although I've met more who claim that than common sense suggests I should have, for some reason!)

Learning styles are the patterns or trends in how we learn – and there are almost as many different models of learning styles as there are researchers into them. What they all have in common, though, is the idea that if you as a teacher or presenter (or even just a general communicator) can find out what someone's learning style is, and present your information in a way that is appropriate for that style, you're more likely to have successful communication.

Think of it as a bit like finding out if someone can read before you give them a book. If they can't, you should probably give them an audio recording instead.

As you can imagine – with education being so important – this is a heavily researched field. The problem lies not in finding the information but in making sense of it.

Fortunately, a lot of the work has been done for us. Back in 2007, Thomas Hawk and Amit Shah (both of Frostburg State University's College of Business) did a review of some of the biggest contenders for 'champion learning style'.

The first of these is Kolb's Experiential Learning Theory from the mid-1980s. Briefly put, Kolb suggested that there were two independent dimensions to learning:

* how a learner ranged from preferring 'concrete experience' to 'reflective observation'
* how a learner scored on a range from 'abstract conceptualization' to 'active experimentation'.

Because the two ideas were independent (orthogonal) they can be drawn on a graph as two lines at right angles, giving four quadrants. Kolb suggested that learning worked best if the process of learning passed through all four of those quadrants and that everyone did that – but they found different quadrants easier to work in than others. (Yes, I know it would be easier to do that with an image, bear with me!)

Gregorc's Learning Style Model grows, in part, out of Kolb's work and looks pretty similar at first glance. Learners are scored for four scales instead of two:

* abstract to concrete perception
* sequential to random ordering
* deductive to inductive processing
* separative to associative relationships.

So far, so good. What we get to next is perhaps the most well-known of the models, the VARK model. This model suggests that people take in information in one of four ways: visually (Visual), by listening (Auditory), by reading and/or writing (Reading), and by movement or doing (Kinesthetic).

The argument goes that visual learners will take in more of what you're saying if you present them with graphs, images and so on, whereas an auditory learner will cope better if you tell them things, and so on. Let's set aside the obvious limitations of this approach – ask yourself what's the best way to learn to waltz… by seeing it, by being told about it, by reading a book about it, or by taking a waltz class? Some things are just so obviously best taught in one 'mode' that the others seem a bit superfluous. But otherwise it's a very popular model.

And I do mean popular. NLP (neuro-linguistic) practitioners will often make reference to it, for example, and many school teachers will refer to Joe Bloggs as a 'visual learner' for example.

Hawk and Shah's next model is the Felder-Silverman approach, which scores learners on a variety of scales (such as 'sensing to intuitive''; 'visual to verbal'; 'sequential to global'; – although annoyingly not all authors use the same terminology). The Index of Learning Styles, or ILS, gives learners scores on each of these scales. (Anyone familiar with the old-style Myers-Briggs Step 1 psychometric instrument will be more than familiar with the approach and its outputs.)

Finally, comes the Productivity Environmental Preference Survey (fortunately abbreviated to PEPS!) of Dunn and Dunn. The shared surname isn't a coincidence since they're a husband-and-wife team. Their idea is that learners respond differently to five environmental factors:

- environmental (sound, light, temperature, etc.)
- emotional (motivation, etc.)
- sociological (learning alone, in groups, with a partner, etc.)
- physiological (how information is perceived, energy levels at the time of learning, etc.)
- psychological (impulsive vs reflective, etc.).

By the time you've read this far it should be pretty clear that these various models overlap each other, look at different things from each other and – overall – don't really build into a clear pattern. And it's worse than I've implied! For example, in a report from the UK's Learning and Research Centre with the rather literal (and long) title 'Should we be using learning styles? What research has to say to practice', the authors have a list of 70 models. At the end of it all, they are somewhat underwhelmed. When compared to other things that have an effect on how much positive change can be attributed to different types of change (all interventions make a positive change – it's just the effect of an intervention taking place!), learning styles have pretty much no effect whatever in the classroom.

Other reviews have been even less kind, suggesting that some of the claims about learning styles (in this context the VARK model) are 'bordering on the absurd'. Three researchers from no lesser establishments than Imperial College, the University of Southampton and the University of Exeter went so far as to use very un-academic words: 'perhaps an over-rated phenomenon, one offering no diagnostic or pedagogical power whatsoever, and one with no independently verifiable claim to validity and reliability'. They're not sitting on the fence here.

All this expert opinion is fine, but at first sight, learning styles have a lot going for them – they seem to make an intuitive, comfortable kind of sense. To make that point, consider the description I made of the Kolb learning style earlier on. Some of you no doubt found it hard to get sorted out – but what if I'd presented the information visually, like the diagram here. Would it have made it easier?

For some of you it probably would, which suggests that you're visual learners, from the VARK model (or that this idea was better given visually for everyone, anyway).

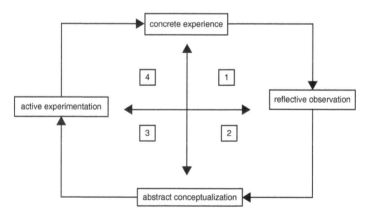

So why doesn't it 'work'? And can we build anything from this into how we make presentations?

Perhaps the answer lies in empirical analysis of preferences, when you measure them. Let's take the VARK model as an example, because it's arguably the most popular and easiest to get data for... Back in one of the early pieces of research, Fleming (the researcher behind much of the VARK model) found that less than half of his subjects had a preference for one mode or another. More than a quarter had a preference for two styles, nearly a tenth for three styles and about a fifth for all four styles. Quite how one can have a 'preference' for more than one thing out of four is a little beyond me, but the main point is that because so many people have so many different modes-of-preference, any effect of using VARK in how you communicate is bound to be diluted.

And the blurring of lines between people with different preferences is substantiated in later work, too. Medics are big on using 'evidence-based this...' and 'evidence-based that...'. Given what they do, that's quite right, too, I believe. And given that medical students learn to stick needles and tubes in patients by practising on themselves and on each other, it seems likely that they're up for being used as research guinea-pigs. What that means for us is that there's a lot of research using medical students.

One such bit of research looked at the learning-style preferences of first-year students at the Wayne State University School of Medicine, where two researchers, Heidi Lujan and Stephen DiCarlo tested the VARK preferences of 250 students. If we're looking for a silver bullet of how to make presentations, in terms of what mode of communication to use, the results were disappointing. Only about a third of students showed a single preference!

Of those in the two-thirds who preferred multi-modal communication, nearly half (43.4 per cent) preferred all four modes of communication.

The idea that people have one learning style or another is, it seems, fanciful – but the idea that using them in our presentations might still be useful, if for no other reason than it makes our presentations more interesting by making us think in a wider variety of ways.

## So what are the big takeaways here?

- **Don't panic.** Don't get hung up on having to customize the way you say everything to everyone. There's no way you can and there's little point trying either.
- **That said, use different styles of delivery if you can.** Even if the benefits are marginal there's no real harm (except to your state of mind, perhaps).
- **For each point you want to make, consider the best way to explain it – in terms of what learning style to use – and use that.** Let the content be your guide, less so your audience. Use movement to explain dance moves, for example, not an audio description.

## Sources

Hawk, T. F. & Shah, A. J. (2007), 'Using Learning Style Instruments to Enhance Student Learning', *Decision Sciences Journal of Innovative Education*, Vol. 5 No. 1 pp 1–19

Coffield, F., Moseley, D., Hall, E. & Ecclestone, K. (2004), 'Should we be using learning styles? What research has to say to practice', *Report of the Learning & Skills Research Centre*

Sharp, J. G., Byrne, J. & Bowker, R. (2007), 'The trouble with VAK', *Educational Futures*, Vol. 1 pp 76–93

Fleming, Neil D., *Teaching and learning styles: VARK strategies* (Christchurch, New Zealand, 2001)

Lujan, H. L. & DiCarlo, S. E. (2006), 'First-year medical students prefer multiple learning styles', *Advances in Physiology Education*, Vol. 30 No. 1 pp 13–16

## See also

Chapters 9, 37 and 6 – Learning styles (or the lack of them!) means you don't have to take them into account when you design diagrams (see **Diagram design**), but there are other things to think about. See **Moving pictures** and **It's not what you say, it's the way that you say it**

## Further reading

There's a really simple (and short!) myth explosion about learning styles on wired.com at http://www.wired.com/2015/01/ need-know-learning-styles-myth-two-minutes/?utm_ content=bufferd56f6&utm_medium=social&utm_source=twitter. com&utm_campaign=buffer. While you're at wired.com it's worth looking at quite a few of the other blog posts; to be honest, it's often worth the time invested.

If you'd rather see it on video, from a professor of psychology, check out https://www.youtube.com/watch?v=sIv9rz2NTUk (Wouldn't it be lovely if YouTube allowed for nicer names to the pages you needed rather than random letters and numbers!)

# 34 WRITING DOWN YOUR WISDOM

*How should you encourage your audience to take notes?*

I've lost count of the number of times someone has said to me something like 'I can't come tomorrow: can you email me your presentation instead?'. Inevitably the answer is 'no': usually it is a polite version of 'no' but it's always 'no'. Why? Because my slides (which are after all the only things I can email) simply don't make much sense if you haven't been there. As you'll have gathered from other chapters, slides that contain sufficient information to make sense on their own make for bad slides and bad presentations.

But there's another, less obvious, reason why I say 'no', which is to do with the person's response to the presentation. It's to do with how they take notes. I've never heard of anyone going through my slides when I've emailed them and doing anything other than giving them a cursory glance over coffee or on the bus – and that's no way to treat my wisdom. Without engaging just a little more than that you're unlikely to take anything in and if you don't take anything in, why waste your time even glancing at my slides, waste the paper printing them or the spare electrons emailing them?

My personal experience is that one of the best ways for people to engage with a presentation is to take notes. Even if the notes themselves get lost or don't make sense, the process of making the notes, it seems to me, fires up parts of the brain in ways that make engagement, understanding, recall and application all the more likely. But that's my personal bias, so take it with a pinch of salt.

What's less personal is the observation that more (and more frequent) note-taking is being done directly to laptops, rather than longhand, and there are certainly logistical advantages of this. I've even done it myself (using a package called Evernote, usually) when I've needed to have things available online or in another office. But I've always felt slightly guilty doing it, because I know that for me at least, I'm only capturing a tiny amount of the information I'm being given and when I'm using my laptop I'm not concentrating as hard on the presentation itself.

Am I typical in that? Some recent research takes on that very question. Previous research has pinned down a number of things pretty clearly:

- people tend to believe that using laptops for note-taking is beneficial
- people admit that laptops are a distraction, but believe that the benefits outweigh the disadvantages
- students using laptops don't concentrate as much as students who aren't using them
- students using laptops have a lower academic performance, overall
- people using laptops tend to be less satisfied with presentations than those who don't.

That seems to be a pretty comprehensive argument *against* using laptops. Most of the research about how to take notes in presentations has tended to concentrate on the risk of the laptop being a distraction, either because it puts temptation in the way of the note-taker or because the mental effort of using the laptop reduces how much head-space people have to concentrate on the content. There are no surprises there, given what we know on who can multitask (almost no one) and what happens to performance on tasks when we try to (it goes down – considerably). There is a bigger question, however, of whether the actual way the laptop is used is a problem: certainly having material recorded is beneficial but there is the question of how the material is processed in order to be recorded.

In short, there are two ways to take notes. You can either take 'generative' notes (by jotting down summaries or paraphrasing etc. – my personal favourite is to use concept mapping) or 'non-generative'. Non-generative note-taking is, essentially, more or less taking down verbatim what is said and obviously it doesn't need as much thought. In short, you can more or less do non-generative note-taking in autopilot mode. On those occasions I've done it, I've told myself I was doing it so that I could engage in more generative activity later, perhaps over coffee.

In the recent study, 33 women and 33 men (and 1 unknown!) were participants and were shown five TED talks of about 15 minutes in length, which they hadn't seen beforehand. (If you've never visited the TED website, I urge you to do so, but not unless you've got a couple of hours of your life to set aside in stunned fascination.) The participants were also given full-size laptops with no Internet access and notepads so that they could take notes in the same manner that they normally did.

Afterwards, the participants were given something to do to distract them (so that they couldn't revise what they'd just seen) for about half an hour before being given a test to cover both factual recall and how well they could apply what they'd learned. The results were clear. There wasn't a difference between the people who'd used notebooks for note-taking and those people who'd used laptops for the questions aimed at testing how well participants could remember facts. On the grounds that the laptop-based notes were more generally available because they could be shared online or emailed to other people, it's score one for the high-tech option.

However, for questions designed to look at how well people could understand and apply what they'd learned ('conceptual-application questions', in the jargon of the paper) the participants who had taken notes on the laptops scored significantly lower than those who'd used longhand techniques.

As a presenter, it's clear to see that if you want people to be able to apply what you're talking about, you should encourage them to take longhand notes. Of course, if it's just a matter of some simple facts to get over it's less important, but over the years I've found a number of different techniques are pretty useful:

- simply ask people not to use their laptops: you can explain that it's to help them make better notes. As we know people will tend to not believe you, so I often give another reason for the suggestion/request as well as that

- reassure people that the slides will be downloadable after the presentation in .pdf format, so that they don't need to panic about getting it all down. My slides tend to not be useful in this context, of course, so what I actually give people is a document that contains the details of what I've been talking about, or even a free book etc.
- make it logistically easy to take longhand notes if it's practical: desks or armrests with note-taking space built in are great for this
- provide something to prime people to make longhand notes, such as a document I've written that contains headings related to each section of the presentation with space under it, blank bullet points to fill in if I'm going to go through a list of things, or even small pictures taken from the appropriate slide... anything, in fact, to stress that note-taking is the norm and to make it easy for people.

You might need to do just a little bit of extra work to set this kind of thing up, but I've always found it to be worthwhile.

Back in the research it transpired that people who worked long hand wrote less down (unsurprisingly, perhaps) but what they did write down had far less literal, verbatim overlap with the presentation. What's more, the more of this processing that the presentation notes contained, the better the person who'd taken those notes performed in the test. What might be a bit more surprising, however, is that when a variation on the original experiment ran, this time encouraging people who chose to use laptops to not take verbatim notes, things improved only marginally.

Of course, all this might not matter if people go back to their notes at a later date. In fact, as laptop-based note-takers take more comprehensive notes, we might expect them to do better if they've had an opportunity to study those notes. In a third experiment, when people were given ten minutes to study their notes a week later, the results flew in the face of this. In fact, participants who had the opportunity to study their longhand notes came out better than any other group in the study, including those who studied their own laptop-based notes.

It seems I was fooling myself about the advantage of reviewing my laptop notes over coffee anyway, so there's no loss in the fact I never got around to it.

## So what are the big takeaways here?

- **Encourage longhand note-taking by providing facilities for it,** such as pads, pens and even structured documents to guide the note-taking.
- **Reassure people who are anxious not to miss anything that the details can be downloaded from a document later,** so that they can concentrate on understanding rather than recording. A document or even a recording of the presentation can be handy here.
- **Encourage people to process what you're saying.** You might think about suggesting they fill in the blanks, or note down a personal application of what you're talking about. If you're using a story you might consider using one taken from a very different (but obviously transferable) set of circumstances, so that people have to think about things just a little bit more: analogies as stories are great for this.

## Source

Mueller, P. A. & Oppenheimer, D. M. (2014) 'The Pen Is Mightier Than the Keyboard: Advantages of Longhand Over Laptop Note Taking', *Psychological Science*

## See also

Chapter 28 – Taking notes helps people take in more and concentrate. See **Stay alert** at the back

## Further reading

I'm always impressed by the sheer amount of work involved in delivering and learning at the UK's Open University. Here's some material on how to take better notes: http://www2.open.ac.uk/students/skillsforstudy/notetaking-techniques.php (Note that you might have to create a free account to access all the material.)

I'm not necessarily saying it's a good idea to print your slides for people to make notes on, but if you want to, the best way to do it in PowerPoint® is to print them several to a page, see: https://support.office.microsoft.com/en-gb/article/Print-your-slides-or-handouts-of-your-presentation-194d4320-aa03-478b-9300-df25f0d15dc4?CorrelationId=0097251b-3d8f-40cb-8f79-57e61d88d163&ui=en-US&rs=en-GB&ad=GB. Or – more realistically – use the Help facility.

It's easier in Keynote®, Apple's equivalent to PowerPoint®, see http://lifehacker.com/353669/print-nine-slides-per-page-in-keynote

# 35 BLINDNESS ISN'T IN THE EYES

*Can your audience pay attention to what you want them to?*

In the almost certain knowledge that you won't take this advice (or can't), I'm going to make a recommendation that will almost certainly have my editor spluttering into her coffee: stop reading this book and get hold of a copy of a book by Christopher Chabris & Daniel Simons. It contains many salient lessons not just about presenting but about life in general and how much we can trust ourselves. Still here? Excellent!

> I've carefully not included the title here as I don't want to give anything away, but to avoid the spoilers later in this chapter you might want to stop here and go online to the first website in the Further reading part of the chapter... As the title of the website gives it away, get someone else to key it in for you...

The book is a thoroughly readable write-up of lots of research with a particular emphasis on two ideas – 'inattention blindness' and 'change blindness'. You can probably guess what they're about already from just those phrases and the title of this chapter. Inattention blindness is our (very human) tendency not to notice things that we're not looking for. That's pretty much what the original experiments with the 'invisible' (or at least unnoticed) gorilla said.

Change blindness is similar – it's our (also very human) tendency not to notice when things change.

The original experiments were wonderfully entertaining – if you've gone to the video already you'll know what I'm talking about. Participants were shown a video of two groups of students playing basketball in front of some lifts with a little graffiti and so on, then told to count the number of times players wearing white passed the ball to each other. To do that you had to concentrate and make a conscious effort to ignore the movement of the other team dressed in black (conveniently). As for many other psychology experiments the real thing being tested wasn't what people were told was being tested, because the actual number of passes wasn't relevant – it was just something to give people to do to occupy their brains.

The really interesting thing was whether or not the participants, while they were concentrating on counting and hence filtering out other things, noticed the gorilla. What gorilla? Well, about two thirds of the way through the video a female student dressed in a full gorilla suit walked across the playing area, turns to the camera and beats her chest and then continues to walk out of frame. In doing so she nearly walks into one of the players and yet about half the participants in the study didn't notice her.

I'm a 'spotter' so like all other spotters when I was told that I was amazed and responded with the usual response of something like 'You're kidding! How can you miss a great big gorilla!?'. Non-spotters respond with equal incredulity about the very presence of the gorilla. (Before you start to worry or do the obvious mental extrapolation, there's no significance that anyone has found to whether you're a spotter or not. Much though I'd like to pretend there is, there's no evidence that being a spotter means I have a higher IQ or anything else.)

What's important in the real world is that this kind of inattention blindness can account for people not noticing critically important clues in crimes (such as the beating of an undercover police officer as reported in the book); car accidents (as drivers fail to notice things like motorbikes); surgical instruments left inside bodies; and so on. The list is endless.

From a presenter's point of view, it's pretty obvious that this means you can't rely on your audience to notice things. You've got to spell things out to them. I can't count the number of times I've worked with people who felt that a specific and unavoidable conclusion was obvious from their slides and who were almost indignant that their audience 'must be stupid' not to have noticed. What's obvious to you is not obvious to other people.

What's even more striking is that when you make it harder for people to concentrate their ability to notice things dramatically reduces. In follow-up experiments, participants were told to count the passes made by both the team in white and the team in black. Gorilla-spotting fell by about 20 per cent! In terms of your presentation, take a moment to think of all the new information you're giving your audience. Remember, particularly, that it's information that's new to them: just because you've known it for years doesn't mean they have. After all, you're the expert, by definition. (By the way, if you don't know more than your audience, why are you giving the presentation?)

Don't leave it to your audience to figure out their own conclusions. Many of them simply can't, because they won't spot your equivalent of the gorilla – the 'blindingly obvious' piece of information or conclusion that they can't fail to miss... except that they do!

Some of the work on change blindness is even more fun. You've probably been stopped on the street by someone to do a customer survey, I imagine. What if halfway through that conversation you lost sight of the interviewer because someone carried a large object between the two of you for a few seconds. Would you notice

> On the up side, what this research might also imply is that what *you* feel is a screamingly obvious, embarrassingly cringe-making mistake is completely overlooked by people in your audience.
>
> Just ask any actor who's fluffed a line.

if the interviewer had changed to another person? Other than the person involved having a map and asking for directions, that's pretty much the experiment we're talking about here and – guess what – only about half the people in the experiment noticed that the person they were talking to had changed. And before you get like me, saying to yourself: 'I'd not fall for that', you should know that a follow-up experiment involving students who'd just had a lecture about this kind of thing, and said precisely that kind of thing, also showed the same pattern. When their details were being taken for an experiment, the administrator they were talking to bent down to deal with some paperwork, only to be replaced. You can guess the results, I'm sure.

In other words, people see what they expect to see, once they've got the pattern set in their heads. If you don't believe me, try proof-reading your own book; you only read what you meant to write, not what you've actually written.

I can personally testify to the power of this effect, quite literally as I write this. On a Christmas trip to my mother's house, I expected to change trains at Birmingham New Street and completely failed to notice that my ticket said I needed to change at Birmingham Moor Street. I read what I expected to read, not the reality.

As a presenter, you can use this information pretty easily. Once you've got your audience thinking and behaving in a certain way, they'll continue to see what they expect to see and hear what they expect to hear. Of course, there's a down side to this habit, too, because they'll continue to see what they expect to see, even if you're trying to get them to see something else. As most presentations (almost by definition) involve giving people information that they are likely to find challenging, confusing or at least different this can have pretty significant implications. It's really important that you make things very explicit to your audience, particularly if you're giving them any information or conclusions that they might not be expecting. Once you draw their attention to it, they'll no doubt wonder why you commented on the obvious – but that's better than not noticing it at all. By definition, things are only obvious once you've seen them.

## So what are the big takeaways here?

- **Don't assume your audience will notice things.** Just because it's obvious to you doesn't mean it is at all obvious to anyone else. In fact, the more unusual it is, the more likely it is that people won't spot it for themselves, so make sure you draw attention to what you need your audience to spot.
- **Don't worry about mistakes.** Your audience almost certainly won't notice them. After all, if they don't notice people changing places in the middle of conversations, why would they notice you mis-speaking something relatively trivial?
- **Make a point of drawing your audience's attention to anything that may be counter to what they expect.** People see what they expect to see, so if you need to get people thinking differently you need to be overt about it. Subtlety has very little place in a presentation, sometimes.

## Source

Chabris, Christopher & Simons, Daniel, *The Invisible Gorilla And Other Ways Our Intuition Deceives Us* (Harper Collins, New York, 2011)

## See also

Chapter 4 – This chapter looks at how we miss things that are presented to us. To see the opposite of that, try **Repeating yourself**

## Further reading

You might want someone else to type this in for you as it rather gives things away – don't say I didn't warn you! www.theinvisiblegorilla.com

You can easily keep up to date with stuff from the guys behind the Invisible Gorilla research on Twitter: https://twitter.com/invisgorilla

It's not just in presentations that the Invisible Gorilla raises his, her or its head. It's a security issue too: http://www.cmu.edu/news/stories/archives/2013/november/nov4_reducingscreeningmistakes.html

In fact, it applies to just about everywhere that professional observation is necessary, such as lifeguards, doctors/nurses and police officers.

# 36

# MINDING WHAT YOU SAY

*Does mindfulness help your nerves?*

Mindfulness is a pretty 'big thing' at the minute. It has its origins in the ancient traditions of Buddhism but the 'modern' version of it is often ascribed to the work of Jon Kabat-Zinn, in the late 1970s, and based at the Massachusetts Medical School. Now that it's firmly established in the mainstream, a lot has been claimed for it, including being able to calm nerves. (Other uses range from helping with clinical depression, to improving the attention of school pupils in class, to helping transplant patients get better sleep!)

Given that making presentations is very often a pretty stressful situation, likely to create a lot of nerves, it's worth looking at it as a tool for presenters. Unfortunately, if there's some validated research out there about the advantages of using mindfulness as a tool like that, I've not found it – although there has been a lot written in less formal routes. And I really do mean a lot. Some of it is more or less robust than other bits: much of it is simply the wolf-in-sheep's-clothing of marketing-dressed-as-educational-material.

Part of the problem lies in the definition of mindfulness. By its very nature it can be hard to pin down. Putting various definitions together, however, brings up something that looks like this:

- it's about becoming consciously aware of things – the antithesis of doing things on auto-pilot
- doing this in a non-judgemental way.

There's a lot of other stuff around those definitions, particularly the first, where the assumption is that what you become aware of is yourself and/or your immediate surroundings. Typically a 'mindful person' (which sounds vaguely silly when you read it like that) focuses on (say) their breathing or what they're eating but the important thing is to do whatever you're doing (or seeing or hearing, etc.) 'mindfully'. If other thoughts intrude, simply acknowledge them, let them pass, and refocus back on the object of your efforts.

Like many things, its simplicity disguises how difficult it actually is. If you want another example, consider the simplicity of losing weight: eat less, move more. Then consider how hard it is to actually lose weight. As a result, it's often regarded as something to develop as a habit, not as a one-off act. Trying only once is likely to lead to limited success: as they say, 'practice makes perfect'.

Despite the sad lack of research into the use of mindfulness for presenters, there's a plethora of research into other fields with implicitly high levels of stress associated with them. With caveats and some caution it might be possible to generalize this research to speaking in public. An example of one such investigation, which pretty much agrees with the rest of the literature, was published in 2013 by Yu Chen, Xueling Yang, Liyuan Wang and Xiaoyuan Zhang. Presumably because they were experimenting on nurses, they published in *Nurse Education Today*.

The core of their research can be summed up like this:

1. The authors selected nursing students at random by email
2. Some of these students replied, agreeing to participate in the research
3. These volunteers were screened and unsuitable candidates were removed
4. The remaining volunteers were split randomly into two groups ('Case' and 'Control')
5. Measurements were taken
6. The 'Case' group was given a week of mindfulness training and support
7. Measurements were taken again
8. The measurements were statistically analysed.

Like all apparently simple research there's quite a lot of detail hidden in that bald description, some of which is obvious. (For example, nursing students might be particularly unusual and nothing like presenters and speakers but for now let's assume that there isn't such a problem.) The third item in the process is interesting because volunteers were not only screened for diagnosed, existing mental health problems but they were also screened according to whether they were currently using psychoactive medication; currently undergoing anything like psychotherapy; had heart issues such as hypertension; and/or had any previous experience in meditation.

The last point is useful for speakers and presenters, because it implies that whatever effects were noted – if any were found, that is – they were down to the intervention in this experiment, making it easier to see how we can use it ourselves. Also interesting is the fact that none of the participants in this research had religious beliefs (Christian, Buddhist, Catholic, Islamic, Taoist): again that implies that any results are the effect of this research.

The sixth point in the process is reassuring, too, as it implies that things can be learned relatively quickly. The research involved only 30 minutes per day. For novices to mindfulness, like me, that's great news, because it implies that it's not a great mystery that takes years and years of dedicated study in a hidden Tibetan monastery while you only re-enter the real world once every four years. Well, I suppose it might be that too, but importantly it means it's something that can be useful relatively quickly and easily with just a little determination. (There are even smartphone apps for it!)

With all those caveats and observations in mind, the good news is that the results were handy for presenters – in short, mindfulness helped.

It's not just in the world of education that mindfulness has been tested – there are dozens of pieces of research from all kinds of environments, including the world of work. One example, which has the added advantage of not just looking at mindfulness but comparing it to yoga to give a bigger picture, was published in 2012 by a research collaboration: Ruth Wolever (and her six collaborators) noted that as well as being more likely to be ill and unhappy, stressed people were more likely to make mistakes and less able to learn – both of which can have an impact upon presenters!

Volunteers (remember, this is in a work environment) were accepted if they scored relatively highly for self-reported stress and excluded if they already did yoga, smoked heavily, took regular medication such as beta-blockers, had one of a number of psychological disorders, had a heart condition, and so on. It's quite an extensive list, designed to make sure nothing interfered with the possible effects of the research. That said, the resulting sample was regarded as pretty representative in terms of demographics and income, etc., so the rejection process didn't appear to be too much of a problem in that regard.

Now followed one of two interventions. Participants either went into a programme of yoga, which lasted one hour per week for 12 weeks, or a 12-week (14-hour) training programme of mindfulness. From their point of view as presenters, the simplicity of the interventions are good news – almost everyone can set aside 12 or 14 hours to learn a new technique that's going to be useful for the rest of our lives. (If that was as easy as I've just made it sound, of course, it would be a lot easier to lose weight, get fit and drink less alcohol, but you know what I mean, I'm sure.) That's especially true because for half the participants, the intervention was done via an online course – there wasn't even a live class to attend.

There was some pretty heavy-duty statistical analysis involved at the end, not least because there were a lot of variables to account for because the research covered everything from self-reported stress to productivity to gender to ethnicity to blood pressure – either to see if it changed as a result of the intervention or to account for it in case it explained the results. The long and short of it, however, is that there was an improvement, compared to people who hadn't had either intervention, in perceived stress and sleep problems for both types of intervention as well as a host of marginal improvements.

There might be a bit of the so-called Hawthorne effect (see Chapter 7) going on here, but who cares – if it works, it works, even if it's just a placebo.

The weak link in all of this, from my experience, is that at the very time you need most to practise your mindfulness, when you're facing your audience, you're least likely to remember to do so. The very thing that makes you need some support also stops you accessing that support: it's a double whammy. My solution, developed over the years, is to simply include a reminder in my notes at the start of my presentation. I'm a fan of what's called 'Presenter View' (I use Keynote® software but the same function is available in PowerPoint® and so on) in which what I see on my laptop screen includes the image the audience is seeing on the big screen, but also shows me other information, such as notes for that slide. What could be more simple than adding a reminder to your introduction slide, so that as your audience is settling down (and you're showing them a slide with the title and your name on the big screen), you've also got a set of notes on your screen reminding you of your various techniques for controlling your nerves?

## So what are the big takeaways here?

- **Take a mindfulness (or yoga) course.** In the case of the mindfulness course the research evidence I've cited suggested you can even do your learning online, rather than face to face.
- **Practise your mindfulness as part of your preparation for your presentation.** Personally, I try to get just a few minutes away from people before I start to speak.
- **Put a reminder to control your breathing and do your mental exercises in your presentation notes.** There's Presenter View in my software to remind me.

## Sources

Yu Chen, Xueling Yang, Liyuan Wang & Xiaoyuan Zhang (2013), 'A randomized controlled trial of the effects of brief mindfulness meditation on anxiety symptoms and systolic blood pressure in Chinese nursing students', *Nurse Education Today*, Vol. 33 Issue 10 pp 1166–72

Wolever, R. Q., Bobinet, K. J., McCabe, K., Mackenzie, E. R., Fekete, E., Kusnick, C. A. & Baime, M. (2012), 'Effective and Viable Mind-Body Stress Reduction in the Workplace:

A Randomized Controlled Trial', *Journal of Occupational Health Psychology*, Vol. 17 No. 2 pp 246–58

## See also

Chapters 7 and 18 – For other ways of handling presentation nerves, see **Stand up! Stand up!** and **Fit to talk?**

Chapter 27 – For a contrasting (and almost contradictory!) approach see **Fashionable fear**

Chapter 30 – I've also found it useful to rehearse my gestures a little, and that's helped a lot with my nerves. See **Waving not drowning**

## Further reading

The National Health Service (NHS) in the UK has some useful starting points for mindfulness at: http://www.nhs.uk/conditions/stress-anxiety-depression/pages/mindfulness.aspx as does the Mental Health Foundation: http://www.mentalhealth.org.uk/help-information/mental-health-a-z/M/mindfulness and Mind, the mental health charity: http://www.mind.org.uk/information-support/tips-for-everyday-living/mindfulness

There's a fascinating, short video about how useful mindfulness is on the TED website: http://www.ted.com/talks/andy_puddicombe_all_it_takes_is_10_mindful_minutes

Mindfulness grew out of Buddhist meditation. Here's an introduction to Buddhism from the BBC: http://www.bbc.co.uk/religion/religions/buddhism

# 37

**MOVING
PICTURES**

*Do animations help or hinder?*

Once upon a time, Disney ruled supreme. Animated adventures
were its domain. Since then, computers have come along and
now anyone can add things that 'move' to their presentation –
but as someone sage once said: 'just because you can, doesn't
mean you should.' I've seen presentations that gave me motion-
sickness, as animation after animation zipped around the screen
and the whole thing began to look like out-takes from James
Cameron's film *Avatar*.

But I've also seen elegantly used animations that really helped me
get my head around what the speaker was explaining.

So what's the difference between feeling like you're on a bad
fairground ride and seeing something useful? And are those
differences common – or am I unusual? It turns out I'm not at
all unusual in finding some animations helpful and others more
of a hindrance. Back in 2007, Tim Höffler and Detlev Leutner
of the Duisburg-Essen University were looking at exactly that
in a powerful meta-analysis of previous work. Think of a meta-
analysis as bringing together all the various pieces of research in
one big melting pot: it's remarkably useful when there have been
lots of studies, with confusing conclusions or when no pattern
has emerged. Often this is because the individual studies simply
weren't big enough, but by combining them a clearer picture
emerges. Where traditional research uses participants, a meta-
analysis uses a combination of participants from all the previous
research.

Up until this work, the prevailing view was that animations had
no intrinsic advantage over static pictures: any advantage they
conveyed was simply because they contained more information,
not because that information was moving, per se. You might

expect that an animation could help someone sitting through a presentation who can't imagine how something like, say, an internal combustion engine works – an animation could show you the process. On the other hand, once a position in the animation is gone, it's gone - the viewer can't return to it and study it in the same way they can study a static picture.

In their meta-analysis, Höffler and Leutner looked at 57 journal articles but then excluded many of them for a variety of reasons. Some didn't give enough information, for example, while others looked at interactive animations, which they didn't want to be included in the scope of the study. In the end they were left with 26 pieces of research and from these they were able to identify 76 different pair-wise comparisons. A 'pair-wise comparison' in this context simply means that A is compared to B, to see which is bigger, stronger or whatever. In this case it means that things like making a comparison between video-based animations and computer-based ones (that is, things like moving arrows or fading in components), or whether the animation did/didn't have annotations.

As you might expect, the statistical techniques were complicated: a lot of things had to be accounted for because of issues of co-variance (where lots of things are related to lots of other things, statistically). For example, if you're trying to compare A and B, but A correlates with C and B correlates with D, it's hard to tell if what you're seeing is the effect of A-vs-B or C-vs-D. That said, the overall results were clear. In 54 of the 76 pair-wise comparisons, the animated option was the best and only twice (out of the 76) was there a statistically significant advantage to the static option.

Life is never that simple, unfortunately, because the pattern and sizes of the differences weren't the same. To a scientist, that sets alarm bells ringing in their head because it implies that there is something else going on – and typically that 'something else' will be some kind of confounding variable that hasn't been included in the original analysis. For example, we might correlate children's height with the ability to play football and get a very strong positive relationship – forgetting the confounding effect of age… older children tend to be taller, giving them an advantage on the football field over their smaller/younger opposition.

Remember that there were more than 70 binary comparisons you could make with the data in this meta-analysis? When you start to unpack them all, the first few results will come as no surprise:

- representational animations are significantly better than representational static images
- animations are particularly good when you're showing people how to do something – e.g. a mechanical procedure of some kind
- animations are also useful when you're helping people learn facts or when you're helping them learn to solve problems
- animations that are there for a reason are a lot more useful than animations that are there for decorative effect.

As a presenter, how you use that information should be obvious! For example, you shouldn't use animation just because you can – it has to mean something if it's not to just be a distraction for your audience. After all, people assume that things have meaning and if you're just making something move because it looks good (no matter how good that makes it look!), you're ensuring people spread their attention more thinly for no good reason.

After that list of the obvious, however, here's a few more surprising things:

- video-based animation isn't *necessarily* better than computer-based animation (even once you've excluded the pointless, prettiness-only animations, which tend to be computer-based)
- extra realism in the videos doesn't *automatically* make the animation any more useful – other things are involved too and are probably more important
- while animations are used more than static images, when neither of them have 'signalling cues' this difference is reduced quite a bit. A signalling cue is something such as arrows or a highlight that is included to help people pick up on what's important. For example, if someone shows you a map with a lot of information on it, you can get overwhelmed and not see the symbol for a church… but if those symbols have red circles around them it's *much* easier!

As a presenter, this little lot means that you shouldn't automatically reach for YouTube to show what you need to show: instead, you can consider creating some movement on your own self-drawn diagram. Also it's particularly useful to include some kind of clue to help people focus on the key things that you need them to notice. Given how easy it is to create movement of various objects on a computer screen these days it's not exactly the work of Einstein to get this kind of thing sorted out.

All of this research was based on animation that the presenter controlled; there was no way the audience could control the speed at which the animation ran. I don't know about you, but I often find I need to see something more than once before I get the hang of it. In 2009, three researchers in the United States included this question in an article that explored a lot of design factors for animations, based upon a remarkably thorough literature review. I'm sure it'll come as no surprise to discover that they noted evidence that allowing computer users to stop and start instruction videos meant that people learned better and faster.

As a presenter, you can't always stop and start videos but there are plenty of times when you can. At the very least you can ask your audience if they want to see the video again and skip back to the slide it was on, or replay the video. Both PowerPoint® and Keynote® allow you to control a video in a slide to pause it, for example, so that you can point out things of interest. Not only does this kind of interaction make it easier for audiences to learn what you're showing them, it seems to make it more likely that they want to do so, because it increases their engagement – you change them from passive observers to active participants.

A technique I've often found useful to help with this is to tell my audience what they're to look out for before I show a video. I don't particularly make it too explicit, but a simple suggestion that they note down examples of X or Y so we can talk about it later can be very effective. I'm sure you can think of your own ideas – anything that gives people control and makes them more engaged is handy.

Mind you, don't take it too far, or you'll have your audience trying to rewind you and your whole presentation, which can put you off your stride and undermine your confidence and your credibility.

## So what are the big takeaways here?

- **Don't use animations just for the sake of it.** Everything in your presentation must have a purpose.
- **Consider simplifying your animations to make it easier for your audience to see what you're interested in,** or find some other way to signpost it, such as by highlighting it or adding an annotation. Don't worry about video-quality animation; it's not all that important.
- **See if you can give your audience some ways of actively engaging with the video** rather than just passively sitting there (particularly if the lights are out!).

## Sources

Höffler, T. N. & Leutner, D. (2007), 'Instructional animation versus static pictures: A meta-analysis', *Learning and Instruction*, Vol. 17 pp 722–38

Plass, J. L., Homer, B. D. & Hayward, E. O. (2009), 'Design factors for educationally effective animations and simulations', *Journal of Computing in Higher Education*, Vol. 21 Issue 1 pp 31–61

## See also

Chapter 9 – The chapter **Diagram design** looks at how to create diagrams if you're not going to animate them

Chapter 17 – Animations and moving pictures are discussed more in **The vexed picture question**, which looks at when and how to use non-animated pictures for maximum effect

Chapter 33 – It might be useful to look at how animations work for people as ways of taking in information – see **Learning styles...** except that, as you'll see, it's less useful than you might think

## Further reading

For a fun (but interesting!) example of what animations can do, have a look at this part of the BBC website: http://www.bbc.co.uk/programmes/articles/4FYLvwSKzJ5vwNv9Z9mwbSD/a-history-of-ideas

If you're feeling really brave you can see the impact of recording out of the office as a beach is used as a whiteboard: http://vimeo.com/25979052

There are some nice examples of video to explain things (surgery, in particular) thanks to the University of Washington at: http://www.orthop.washington.edu/?q=media/surgical-examples.html Even though it's only 'cartoons', some of it made me wince. So be warned!

*What font should I use on my slides?*

There's a lot of research on fonts and legibility but there are no clear conclusions – or at least no simple ones. Legibility seems to depend too much on context for that. Given how important passing written information is to how Western societies work, you'd be forgiven for being surprised by that: I was. So what's the problem? There are quite a few:

- research papers tend to be about specific and unusual demographic groups, such as children (for obvious reasons)
- some of the big name researchers in the area have been found guilty of making their results up (seriously!)
- for some reason this is a contentious issue and personal attacks on the reputations of researchers aren't unknown. To complicate things further, of course, these attacks are often disguised as research
- the whole area is so convoluted that it's almost impossible to disentangle the multiple, overlapping metrics for various fonts (x-height vs real height, for example; the length of ascenders and descenders and the size of counters and so on) (And the fact that you probably don't know and don't care what I'm talking about sort of illustrates the point.)
- people don't know what's good for them!

Let me unpack that last point before anyone takes offence. Research by Ole Lund (as part of his PhD work submitted with lovely irony to the University of Reading) suggests that there's no guarantee of a relationship between readers' preferences for fonts and their performance as readers.

To further mess things up, research has tended to concentrate on individual aspects of fonts and has investigated them individually. While that is good scientific protocol, it's not very helpful in the real world. And finally, of course, there's the issue that there's a significant difference between legibility and readability. Legibility is the measure of how easy to read something is but readability is more suited for screeds of text, because it also takes account of things like spacing of letters. One unavoidable consequence of this difference is that while a legible font can be made unreadable by bad spacing, etc. an illegible font cannot be saved by perfect spacing.

For me, this means that legibility is the more important element of the two because for slides we're only talking about a few words at a time. My argument is that if a slide qualifies for a *readability* assessment then there is already more than enough text on it and consequently there are bigger problems to worry about. The slide is already a bad one – as you'll see in other chapters.

In short, academic research doesn't give much guidance in terms of what fonts presenters should use, so it seems we need to look elsewhere for help.

And where better to look than roads? Or, more specifically, road signs. Why? Because road signs are pretty much the epitome of how to give just the right amount of information using the shortest, clearest, and fastest means possible. There's an elegance to road signs (and for that matter railway safety signs) that make them so slick we barely notice them until they go wrong.

In the UK the story pretty much begins back in 1963, with a report to the Department of Transport from the Worboys Committee and the creation of a special font called (appropriately enough) Transport. The changes and recommendations of the report became legal in 1964 and they've been updated semi-regularly since then, most recently in 2002.

If you've ever driven in the UK you've seen the results of all this work and these days the definitive document to refer to is the Traffic Signs Manual from 1982. It's pretty comprehensive,

Is it just me, or does that sound like an agenda for presentations and – particularly – slides? As a presenter, I subject all my slides to the traffic sign test: can it be as easily and quickly grasped as a traffic sign? If not, how can I change it to make it more so?

and appropriately pleasant and easy to read. For example, the Introduction states pointedly that signs must: 'Give road users their message clearly and at the correct time. The message must be unambiguous and speedily understood.'

The manual goes on to say that to do this, signs must have 'correct legibility distance' and that this legibility depends 'mainly on the size of the lettering … although the use of adequate colour contrast … are also important contributory factors'.

And things get pretty detailed with specifications for size, text size, font and colours. For example, it turns out that to make sure letters are spaced the optimum distance apart, they are placed on 'imaginary tiles': all these tiles are the same height but their widths vary, depending on the letter. Presenter take note: for maximum legibility, these tiles are to be twice the height of the lower-case letter x.

In the words of the manual: 'Correct vertical spacing is important; it is the sign designer's equivalent of punctuation.' As a presenter, the implication is clear: if we're designing slides that have text on them it's very (very!) important to have the text clearly vertically spaced – and now we know by how much.

Spacing between words is just as tightly specified, and is to be two and a half times something called the stroke width. What's the stroke width? It's rather obscurely defined as the one quarter the height of the same letter x as used for vertical distances. Still with me?

What this implies for presenters is that you could do a lot worse than to get yourself the Transport font. Be careful though, as it probably isn't available on many other computers. If you export slides to a computer

> I can't count the number of times I've wished a presenter had known how to embed fonts: it's embarrassing to sit there looking at fonts that remind me of a Picasso – and not in a good way.

without the font, you might end up with your beautifully designed slides having that computer's default font foisted on them – probably Garamond, or Times New Roman. Or if the world really hates you it'll be `Courier` or even **Comic Sans**. Whatever it is though, you'll end up having very shoddy looking slides. Better to take your own laptop with you if you're going to use it.

It's not just fonts, either. If you're travelling with your slides, make sure you embed videos, graphics, and so on, otherwise you could be in for a nasty surprise as the new computer can't find them, no matter how hard it tries…

It's probably easier to stick to fonts that look similarly legible but are more readily available; but if you want to use something with a bit more originality, look at PowerPoint®'s ability to 'save' with the fonts you use embedded – that way, the fonts are part of your file and are certain to be available on other machines.

We can get some advice on all of this from safety signs on railways. After all, what's more important than safety signs? Here the key document glories in the title of Document Ref ITL/GN0001. Within it are the specifications that all safety signs are to be in **Helvetica Medium** (which has the advantages of being readily available and is a sans-serif typeface) and should have a ratio of width to character height of 'approximately 1:5.7'. (I have to admit that 1:5.7 doesn't sound very 'approximate' to me.)

To make the signs as legible as possible 'tracking values' (the technical term for how far apart letters are) should be set very specifically:

- characters to be tracked at 22 per cent of the lower case x's character width
- words are to be spaced at 75 per cent.

And just as specifically, the absolute heights of letters are figured out. Admittedly, it's a bit harder for presenters than for railway safety staff, because for safety signs there's a calculated, assumed 'viewing distance', leading to complicated tables where, for each 'viewing distance' there is a specified x-height for each of three types of text (header text such as 'first-aid box', instruction text, and so on).

If the sign is to be viewed at a metre away, header text is to have an x-height of 5.5 mm. At five metres away it's to have an x-height of 13.6 mm and at 10 metres it's 16.7 mm. Presenters will find it harder to stick to that kind of specification, because it's not always possible to figure out how large your text will be on the big screen (projectors have

> One slightly tongue-in-cheek piece of advice I often give clients paraphrases my mum when I was growing up. Whenever I asked for permission to do something her response would be: 'If you have to ask, the answer is "no".' If you are asking yourself 'is my font big enough?', the answer is almost certainly 'no'.

different beam angles and are different distances from the screen etc.) but the point about text sizes being bigger than we ever think they need to be is well made! If in doubt, use bigger fonts on any slides.

It's worth mentioning here that this means your colour schemes for text should be to maximize the contrast between text and background. And if you can't (let's say because your boss insists that grey on pink is a good idea because they are his favourite colours) you need to take account of that by having even bigger text.

## So what are the big takeaways here?

- **Consider your fonts, and the spacing.** Make them bigger than you think you need to and use Helvetica as your default.
- **Think about saving your fonts as part of the file which contains your slides,** so you can be sure that they'll be available on other computers.
- **If the colour contrast between your text and your background isn't ideal,** you need to make your fonts even bigger to compensate.

## Sources

Lund, Ole (1999), 'Knowledge Construction in Typography: The case of legibility research and the legibility of sans serif typefaces', PhD thesis, University of Reading.

Traffic Signs Manual, Department for Transport, Department for Regional Development (Northern Ireland), Scottish Executive, Welsh Assembly Government, published for The Department for Transport under licence from the Controller of Her Majesty's Stationery Office

Document Ref ITL/GN0001, published by the Rail Safety and Standards Board, 2003 – updates are published relatively frequently.

## See also

Chapter 3 – Fonts should be clear and **Clarity is king** in a good presentation

Chapter 24 – **The best of PowerPoint®** reveals other ways to help make things easier for your audience

## Further reading

If you want to download your own copy of the Transport font you're in luck: http://www.urbanfonts.com/fonts/Transport.htm

The website at cbrd.co.uk is a labour of love. Or obsession. Either way there is a very readable (thought somewhat quirky) series of articles about Worboys and road signs: http://www.cbrd.co.uk/articles/war-to-worboys

Fonts seem to attract a degree of nerdiness. People collect them and argue about them in pubs! And write quizzes to see if you can tell them apart. (See http://www.ironicsans.com/helvarialquiz for an example.) My person suspicion is that if you score too highly in arial-vs-helvetica combat you need to get out more.

It's perhaps more important for handouts than slides, where the number of words should be so small it doesn't matter too much, but fonts designed to make things easier to read for people with dyslexia have become more popular recently. Try: http://www.dyslexiefont.com/en/dyslexia-font

People love to hate fonts, because of the belief that you can infer something about a person's personality by what font they use. There might be something in it – just look at logos as you walk down the nearest high street. The BBC did a light-hearted article on it a while ago (http://www.bbc.co.uk/news/entertainment-arts-15253215); while there is a fully tongue-in-cheek answer to the question of what happens if you change the fonts in those logos here: http://www.pixelonomics.com/famous-brands-logos-regular-fonts-regulabrands

If you want to get a bit more nerdy about typefaces, fonts and other things, try *Just My Type* by Simon Garfield (Profile, London, 2011).

# 39 GETTING TO BED

*How important is a good night's rest before the big day?*

We've all been there… the presentation is so important that we feel anxious; and that anxiety makes it harder for us to get a good night's sleep and that – in turn – makes us worry that we're not going to perform well. And if you're anything like me, you enter a vicious spiral of not being able to sleep because you're worrying about the effects of not sleeping… and on… and on…

And for those of us who have to travel for our presentations it can be even harder to get the necessary time in bed.

And, of course, there's always the possibility of the emergency presentation – the one where you're still working on it until the middle of the night. Not that I've ever done that. Oh no. I'm a professional. Honest!

Of course, it's not just presenters who suffer from sleep deprivation problems. Doctors on hospital wards feel it – as does anyone taking an exam. In fact it's such a significant issue that quite a lot of the research involved has been carried out by the army.

But does it really matter? Does a bad night's sleep really mean we're not going to perform well? After all, if the adrenaline surge of performance is good for anything, it's surely good for keeping us going when we're a bit under par.

In 2000, researchers looked at the effects of not sleeping on the exam performance of students. In a very literally entitled paper called 'Moderate sleep deprivation produces impairments in cognitive and motor performance equivalent to legally prescribed levels of alcohol intoxication', they compared the effects of not sleeping with those of drinking alcohol. And on the logic that no serious presenter would stand up to present drunk, if the effects are similar then the implications for presenters of not getting enough sleep could be significant.

They worked with a fairly opportunistic sample of 37 men and 2 women (with a heavy bias towards driving as part of their job or military role) aged between 30 and 49 and, although the participants were picked as much for convenience as for anything else, there wasn't anything particularly unusual about them: they might not be perfectly representative of the 'real world' but they weren't too far off.

After a few practice tests to get the hang of how they worked, participants were given a barrage of tests, picked because their results were expected to be impacted by the effects of fatigue: they ranged from simple vigilance tests to speed-of-response tests, hand-eye coordination tests and so on, up to complicated memory tests. Everyone did the two parts of the research, sleep deprivation and alcohol consumption, in different orders with plenty of rest between the two parts, to make sure biases were minimized. As you might expect, performance in the tests decreased as participants were given more alcohol: for example, by the time blood alcohol concentration had reached 0.05 per cent response speeds had dropped by between 8 and 15 per cent and coordination measures had dropped by about 10 per cent.

For those people who weren't sleeping, by the time they'd had about 13 hours of sleep deprivation their reaction speeds fell by nearly 60 per cent for one of the tests and nearly 30 per cent for tests requiring dual actions. The only good news for presenters is that the tests for grammatical reasoning, memory and search tasks (that is, things to do with *thinking* rather than *doing*) had *only* dropped by up to 10 per cent.

*Only.* But who wants to be 10 per cent below par?

And after 17 hours of sleep deprivation only, performance in tests was as bad as for people who had failed the legal limit of alcohol for driving. And if you'd not be safe to drive, should you be in charge of a data projector?

You're less likely to kill someone with a laptop than a car, I suppose...

Here's an important point for presenters... what perhaps makes this worse is that people suffering from degraded performance because they've not slept don't realize it. I'm speculating that perhaps the first thing to go when you're in that state is your ability to make that kind of judgement, rather like the fool who insists they're a better driver after a few pints at the pub... but I'm speculating...

Researchers June Pilcher and Amy Walters weren't speculating, however, when they looked at exam performance for students. They worked with 65 students and used a cognitive test that was based entirely on significant mental – but not physical – effort and a range of self-reporting tools for capturing things like how much effort participants were putting into their work, concentration, and so on.

Unsurprisingly, after not being allowed to sleep the students who'd been kept awake (can you imagine how annoying it must be to know that half the people in this experiment are getting the same rewards as you but not having to stay awake?!) performed statistically significantly worse than their fresher counterparts. There was also a difference in terms of how well the students thought they were concentrating and how well they'd done in their tests; they self-reported fatigue (no surprise there!) and feelings of confusion and bewilderment.

Interestingly, the sleep-deprived students felt they were concentrating more than the others. They also thought they were working harder – that is, they expended more effort on tasks.

The moral there for presenters is about not knowing what you're doing when you're tired. From the point of view of presenters, the conclusions are obvious: don't stay up late working on your presentation. Instead, do what you normally do to get a good night's sleep. There's plenty of advice online about how to get to sleep. The way I do it personally is to:

- have a checklist of things that can go wrong – and prepare for each one so I know that it won't (for example, I know I've packed a power extension cable, just in case)
- do some light exercise (not immediately before bed!) so that I'm in the right psychological and physiological place to sleep
- have a small evening meal.

At this point, the army comes to the rescue with some research about coping on those occasions when you just can't sleep, and how to keep your performance up. Tracy Rupp and her colleagues carried out a piece of research that was so vicious on the participants it carries a statement about ethical approval which explicitly states the research doesn't breach the 1964 Declaration of Helsinki (a sort of declaration of human rights for research).

Rupp and her colleagues were looking at whether it's possible to 'bank' sleep ahead of when it might be needed. The idea is that if you think you're going to have a bad night's sleep on Friday you might be able to sleep more on the days earlier that week to prepare yourself for it. Using Time In Bed (TIB) as a proxy for actually sleeping, volunteers ranged from 18 to 39 went through:

- 14 days of measurements while they went about their usual activities and slept normally
- 7 days sleeping in the laboratory in one of two groups. The 'habitual' group was the control group who carried on with their normal TIB and the 'extended' group (the experiment group) had a higher TIB
- 7 days of sleep deprivation for everyone
- 5 days of recovery for everyone.

A whole battery of measurements and tests was carried out – so much so that it takes more than one research paper to report it. The long and short of it, however, is that:

- in pretty much every test, people in the 'extended' TIB group did better than the 'habitual' group
- younger volunteers had a greater decline in performance but recovered faster
- people in the 'extended' TIB group recovered faster.

A lot of the tests were for things related to reflexes and physical responses (psychomotor vigilance tasks), which a presenter needs, of course, but there were also tests of how quickly people learned and thought, too. And a presenter who thinks slowly or doesn't put two and two together very quickly isn't going to deliver a great talk.

Fortunately, so long as you're not taken by surprise (and have to deliver that career-making (or career-breaking!) presentation with only a day's notice), you know what to do: be disciplined and get extended TIB.

Simple, really.

## So what are the big takeaways here?

- **Get a good night's sleep.** Easier said than done, I know, but do what you can.
- **Get to bed early for the few days before the night before The Big Day.** Avoid those things that are going to spoil your sleep (tea, coffee and alcohol?) so that you get good quality sleep, too.
- **Remember to take the question of rest seriously and plan for it.** Remember that one of the first things to go is your judgement about how hard you're working and how hard you're concentrating, so get all your planning done (and as much of your preparation as you can possibly manage) before things start to get intense. All you should do on the day is deliver – everything else should have been taken care of!

## Sources

Williamson, A. M. & Feyer, A-M. (2000), 'Moderate sleep deprivation produces impairments in cognitive and motor performance equivalent to legally prescribed levels of alcohol intoxication', *Occupational and Environmental Medicine*, Vol. 57 Issue 10 pp 649–55

Pilcher, J. J. & Walters, A. S. (2010), 'How Sleep Deprivation Affects Psychological Variables Related to College Students'

Cognitive Performance', *Journal of American College Health*, Vol. 46 No. 3 pp 121–6

Rupp, T. L., Wesensten, N. J., Bliese, P. D. & Balkin, T. J. (2009), 'Banking sleep: realization of benefits during subsequent sleep restriction and recovery', *Sleep*, Vol. 32 No. 3 pp 311–21

Rupp, T. L., Wesensten, N. J. & Balkin, T. J. (2010), 'Sleep history affects task acquisition during subsequent sleep restriction and recovery', *Journal of Sleep Research*, Vol. 19 No. 2 pp 289–97

## See also

Chapter 13 – Make sure no one tells your audience you're exhausted from travelling. Get the introductions right in **Being who you are**

Chapter 18 – Along with sleep, try exercise. See **Fit to talk?**

## Further reading

The National Institute on Aging has some good starting-point advice on sleep here: http://www.nia.nih.gov/health/publication/good-nights-sleep. It's only a starting point though!

You'll have to pay for the detailed access, unfortunately, but the JAMA journal *Internal Medicine* gives a lot of information about using mindfulness to help with sleep even in the abstract: http://archinte.jamanetwork.com/article.aspx?articleid=2110998

There's a lot of good stuff about sleep on the TED website. For example, you can discover that our normal sleep cycles don't match what we do now: http://www.ted.com/talks/jessa_gamble_how_to_sleep

# 40 KNOWING HOW GOOD YOUR PRESENTATION WAS

*How do we know how well we've done?*

The chances are that if you're reading this book you're not overly confident as a presenter (or maybe you're just curious, etc.) but let's pretend I can measure how good you are as a presenter *and* how good you think you are – the two aren't necessarily the same. In fact, the chances are that these two figures would be badly correlated with each other – and not correlated in an interesting and predictable way.

There are lots of research papers in this field but one of particular note was published in 2003, by David Dunning, Kerri Johnson, Joyce Ehrlinger and Justin Kruger. The effect discussed in the paper has become known as the Dunning-Kruger effect and it can be summed up like this:

*People are bad judges of how good they are at something and the worse they are at it, the worse they are at judging that fact.*

What Dunning and Kruger found (repeatedly, in different pieces of research, along with lots of other people) is that:

- people generally estimate how good they are at something rather optimistically
- people who are poor at something overestimate their ability, skill, knowledge, etc. by a considerable margin
- people who are relatively good at things tend to slightly underestimate how good they are.

What that results in is the impossible idea that everyone thinks they're above average. To put it more colloquially, dumb people are too dumb to know they're dumb. Think about that before you answer the question I posed at the top of this chapter – how good a presenter are you really?

I've been a professional public speaker for many years now and I think I'm pretty good – I certainly think I'm one of the better ones around – but that, the Dunning-Kruger effect predicts, is exactly what I would say, whether or not I'm any good. What that means as a presenter is that you can't judge your own skills, abilities or, crucially, your own presentations.

Dunning and Kruger suggest that there are two explanations for the effect, which have an impact at different ends of the skills-spectrum. People at the bottom end of the spectrum don't have the skills to carry out whatever they're being asked to do and therefore, by definition, they don't have the skills to accurately assess whether they're doing it well or not. The example they give is of people with poor grammar skills: in order to know you're not good at grammar you need, by definition, to know what the correct grammar is for any given sentence.

On the other hand, people at the top end of the spectrum, the ones who slightly underestimate their performance, do so because they are more acutely aware of what's going on. Statistically, these misjudgements at the top end of the spectrum aren't nearly so marked as at the bottom however.

One particular irony of this is that it makes it very difficult to see what to do about any situation since those who need to improve are unable to see that they need to do so: otherwise they'd not be in the position of needing to improve in the first place.

One implication for presenters is that there's a chance that if we think we're 'bombing out', we're possibly just more aware of our weaknesses than other, brasher, more confident speakers. In any case, I'd assert that you can't measure how good a presentation is by how it went at the time – you measure success by how much effect it has afterwards.

Dunning and Kruger's work – and pretty much all the work that's followed – has been based on comparing people's predictions of how well they'd do in tests of some kind (either intellectual or more pragmatic, such as knowing which end of a gun is which) with how well they actually did. What's particularly interesting here is that how well people concluded that they'd done on any specific test is:

- badly correlated to how well they *actually* did
- very strongly correlated to how well they *thought* they were going to do.

In other words, people who think they're good at something tend to believe they've done pretty well at any given attempt at whatever it is, irrespective of the objective data. Dunning and Kruger's term for this was 'top-down performance estimates'.

Of course scientists being scientists meant it wasn't long before different explanations of what Dunning and Kruger had observed started to surface. It's possible, for example, that the whole thing is a statistical artefact – if everyone overestimates how good they are at things, then the apparent ability to predict how good we are has to be more accurate towards the top end of the spectrum, precisely because it is the top end of the spectrum. We can't predict we'll get higher scores than 100 per cent right.

Let's take an example of this. Instead of creating an impression of how quickly a person solves crosswords by building up an impression from lots of times when they've solved crosswords, people tend to have a preconceived notion of how good they are – and to adjust their perception of how quickly they solved any given crossword in accordance with that initial set of assumptions!

Ironically, the more you think that doesn't apply to you, the more it might!

Alternatively, measures of performance might be so poor that the whole thing is a fallacy.

To cut a long story short, there's a lot of evidence that Dunning and Kruger's original ideas were largely supported by the evidence. Experiments have been run on everything from how well students believed they would/did do in an exam to how well people would/did perform in a test about guns or how well they and their team performed in debating competitions. Some of the statistical analysis and meta-analysis of data gets petty high-powered pretty quickly. Overall, however, there's a lot of support for Dunning and Kruger.

As an irritating aside, recent research published in the online journal PLOS ONE in August of 2014 rubs salt into the raw wound. Researchers Lamba and Nityananda point out that people who overestimate their own abilities are also likely to be overrated by observers and under-confident people are likely to be underrated. If you put this together with the Dunning-Kruger effect you get the perfect storm of people who aren't very good at something believing they are and having that belief supported by the beliefs of others, who also believe they, in turn, are high-flyers.

One possible area that's worth exploring for the original Dunning-Kruger effect is that people who were performing fairly poorly on any given measure knew they were doing poorly, but simply couldn't admit it, presumably to themselves as well as to other people. Some experiments that have given people incentives to make more accurate predictions have not made much impact upon whatever is going on in these people's minds.

In later work, working with others, Dunning and Kruger found that giving their poor performers some training improved their ability to predict things, which suggests that there's a glimmer of hope: by *knowing* that things can be improved, they can in fact *be* improved. Skills and even things like intelligence are malleable.

But just for fun, go back and ask yourself how good you are, really, at presenting. Are you sure?

## So what are the big takeaways here?

- **Remember that if you feel that a presentation has gone badly it might be that it actually went well** and you're just the kind of presenter who is attuned to what has gone wrong and is aware of the things you could have done to make it go better. (Of course, there's the question of how you should interpret a presentation that you think has gone well... has it really? Or are you just so bad at judging your ability to make presentations that you don't realize it?)
- **Act as though you're sure of yourself.** You can convince other people that you're good at something simply by acting as though you are. While you can't fool all of the people all of the time, you can probably fool most of the people most of the time – but remember how the story of *The Emperor's New Clothes* finishes! And in all cases, make sure you're acting ethically. And at the very least, don't allow your uncertainties to show, because other people will judge you by them.
- **Remember that skills are learnable and that even something as apparently innate as intelligence is largely the result of certain mindsets.** By believing that you can become a better presenter, you open the way to becoming a better presenter – it's not simply a skill set you are born with/without.

## Sources

The original work by the authors Dunning and Kruger was published a little earlier, in 1999, and other research in the field is earlier still.

Dunning, D., Johnson, K., Ehrlinger. J. & Kruger, J. (2003), 'Why People Fail to Recognize Their Own Incompetence', *Current Directions in Psychological Science*, Vol. 12 No. 3 pp 83–7

Lamba, S. & Nityananda, V. (2014), 'Self-Deceived Individuals Are Better at Deceiving Others', *PLOS ONE* Vol. 9(8): e104562

## See also

Chapter 21 – For another example of when people don't know what's best for them, have a look at **Being more persuasive** – particularly looking at the work of the Nudge Unit.

## Further reading

The Nudge Unit, or more properly The Behavioural Insights Team, is now an independent organization, with an interesting blog: http://www.behaviouralinsights.co.uk/blog

If you're competent the Dunning-Kruger effect suggests you're aware of your mistakes, how about getting stuck in the negatives… https://www.youtube.com/watch?v=7XFLTDQ4JMk

# INDEX

teaching, 62–6
testosterone, 37, 39, 40
text:
  complexity, 13–17
  fluency, 15–16
text-image balance, 99–102, 112
tongue-twisters, 153
Traffic Signs Manual, 228–9
transfer tests, 110, 113
Transport font, 228, 229, 232
trust, 71, 183–6

variation in delivery, 26, 64
VARK model, 197, 199–200
vocal warm-up, 152–3

white noise, *see* background noise
working memory, 7–8, 81–5, 91, 100, 139, 156, *see also* memory; retention

x-height, 229–31

# GENIUS

**Bring a little genius into your day.**

# SO MUCH OF WHAT YOU'VE BEEN TOLD ABOUT BUSINESS IS WRONG . . .

Too many theories, not enough real-world evidence. The *Genius* series cuts through the noise to bring you proven research from around the world that you can use to reach your goals at work.

INNOVATIVE: *Genius* is the only series of business books that is based on actual research, rather than the opinions and preconceptions of the author.

IN-DEPTH: Our authors have read thousands of journal articles, books and pieces of research, so that you don't have to. The 40 most compelling insights each form a chapter of their *Genius* title.

PRACTICAL: As well as explaining the research, the *Genius* series shows you practical ways to implement these in a business setting.

UNRIVALLED: Our authors are leading authorities in their respective fields – their teachings will improve your work and business skills.

# COMING SUMMER 2015

**ISBN:** 9781473615007
**RRP:** £12.99, Paperback

**ISBN:** 9781473605367
**RRP:** £12.99, Paperback

**ISBN:** 9781473605381
**RRP:** £12.99, Paperback

## ABOUT THE BOOKS

Presentation, sales and strategy are topics surrounded by myths and received wisdom, but it doesn't have to be that way. The *Genius* series brings together 40 proven pieces of research in one place and shows how to implement them to achieve success.

## ABOUT THE AUTHORS

**Simon Raybould** is a speaker and trainer. As a speaker, he specialises in resilience, emotional robustness, public speaking and presenting. As a trainer, he is the director of the training company Aware Plus. He worked for 24 years as a university researcher, publishing in many peer-reviewed journals and developing an international reputation.

**Graham Jones** is a leading authority on the science of selling. He is a Member of the British Psychological Society, a Visiting Lecturer at University of Buckingham Business School, and an Associate Lecturer at the Open University. He has written more than 20 books, which have been translated around the world.

**Richard Jones** is a strategic and change management consultant and entrepreneur in the field of telecoms and technology. He has consulted at board and government level on projects from Kazakhstan to Kansas and from Curacao to Colombo. He has co-founded several different companies, one of which was acquired for 45 million GBP, another of which floated on the Nasdaq, and another has now received 50 million USD of investment.

# COMING LATER THIS YEAR

**ISBN:** 9781473609273
**RRP:** £12.99, Paperback
September 2015

**ISBN:** 9781473609105
**RRP:** £12.99, Paperback
December 2015

**ISBN:** 9781473605473
**RRP:** £12.99, Paperback
December 2015

**ISBN:** 9781473605404
**RRP:** £12.99, Paperback
November 2015